MANDEVILLE

D1424478

MATTHEW FRANCIS

Mandeville ⌒

faber and faber

First published in 2008
by Faber and Faber Limited
3 Queen Square London WC1N 3AU

Typeset by Faber and Faber Limited
Printed in England by T. J. International, Padstow, Cornwall
Printed on FSC accredited material

A CIP record for this book
is available from the British Library

ISBN 978-0-571-23927-6

10 9 8 7 6 5 4 3 2 1

For many men desire to hear of unfamiliar things and take pleasure in them.

The Travels of Sir John Mandeville

Contents

Author's Note

The Travels of Sir John Mandeville first appeared in French some time around the middle of the fourteenth century. Though the author claims to be an English knight, nothing is known for certain about his identity, or whether the claims he makes about his life and travels have any substance – though much of his material is undoubtedly derived from other manuscript sources. These poems are based on C. W. R. D. Moseley's modern English version of the text (Penguin Classics), though I have also referred to the Middle English translation known as the Cotton Manuscript in the Dover edition. Barbara W. Tuchman's *A Distant Mirror* and Norbert Ohler's *The Medieval Traveller*, translated by Caroline Hillier, provided valuable information on context. I found the story I used in the first 'On Circumnavigation' poem in an essay by L. Chekin on *www.vitiaz.ru/congress/en/thesis/2.html#_edn22*.

I should like to thank the following for their help and advice: Tiffany Atkinson, Peter Barry, Creina Francis, Richard Francis, Kelly Grovier, Elin ap Hywel, Matthew Jarvis, Richard Marggraf-Turley, Kevin Mills, Elisabeth Salter, Damian Walford Davies, Tim Woods. Acknowledgement is due to the following magazines in which some of these poems first appeared: *New Welsh Review*, *PN Review*, *Poetry Wales*.

Medieval thinkers were well aware that the world is round, though this topographical picture was juxtaposed in their minds with a symbolic one in which Jerusalem was at the centre. I have tried to represent both pictures, and both modes of thinking, in these poems.

Mandeville ✑

Mandeville's Departure

For you must know that the world is round. In its centre
the gold pin of Jerusalem holds down the twelve winds
and the three continents ringed by the Great Sea Ocean.

And our islands on the world's edge are mere gritty dots
in that circling ocean, our shores crumbling into it,
the hills blurry with rain, the shires foundering in mud.

So all who leave them must step on to the up-and-down
of a wooden ship, as I, Sir John Mandeville, did
on Michaelmas Day of the year 1332.

A little town by the shore was my last sight of home.
It was a place that had gone grey staring at the sea,
where nets were draped on the shingle and ropes made their nests.

I felt the sea strain against the carcass of the ship
like the man rolling a barrel on the quay, and watched
as the waves walloped a sunk-in post, half-green, half-dry.

Barnacles were clinging there, the kind that hang from stalks,
and have smooth shells, like eggs – they are called goose barnacles.
Each stalk had a nodule on the end, gripping the post,

like the head and beak of a tiny goose. Underneath,
feathery tails hung down from the shells, skimming the sea.
On dark nights, these outlandish creatures hatch into birds

and fluster up together into the winter air,
splaying out against the clouds in a figure of wings.
Then they are called barnacle geese, and frequent the winds,

as once they did the waves. But they must return to breed.
Under their feathers pulses the slime of a shellfish,
and therefore it is lawful to eat them on fast days.

And if like them you would uproot yourself you must spread
your sails to the twelve winds and cross the Great Sea Ocean,
which is also called Death, for it flows round everything,

so when you enter it you must say farewell to life
and shut yourself up in a box, to welter in death
until it chooses to spit you out or swallow you.

You will make do with dry food, the sawdust of biscuit,
the shrivelled leather of fish, bacon you will dig out
with your fingernails from the crannies between your teeth.

You will come to an accommodation with the rats
that know better than you the way to gnaw a living
and have chewed nests for themselves out of the ship's fibres.

And you will lie in the wooden dark waiting to breathe
the air your companions have used for their snores and farts,
while the night is lifted and dropped with you inside it.

Of Storms

It was Michaelmas when I stepped aboard. On the land
corn warmed the fields, apples thumped into the withered grass,
but the sea knew otherwise. Winter had set in there,

the black clouds rolling under the hull, storms approaching
from far out, under the cover of their own darkness,
and we set sail then, for the place where the storms came from,

and found only a sea of iron dented by rain
and a gentle heaving of its bulk that was answered
by all the fluids in my body seeking their home.

I, Sir John Mandeville, have known many storms at sea,
the mingling of salt and fresh on the face, the shifting
of slabs of solid ocean as if in an earthquake,

I have seen the wall of the horizon come up close
and stand over the ship waiting to topple – sometimes
we burrowed under, and sometimes it fell and pinned us,

but my first voyage was a fair one. After three days
we sighted France crouched under the stained-glass light that
    falls
upon a country that is still nine-tenths a daydream.

Of Circumnavigation

The world is round, and wrapped in the sea like a wet cloak.
Whatever distant islands you travel to, trading
wool for spices, grey sea for blue, our brass sun for gold,

you will find yourself in the end on the brink of home,
like the man washing the coconut flesh from his knife
who let it drop from his fingers over the ship's side,

and slip into the water. He watched it sidle down
past the nudging fish as if it had fins of its own,
and wobble into vagueness. After it passed from view,

the knife plunged through the skylight of his house in England
before his wife's eyes and stuck in the kitchen table.
She knew it at once, and that he was up there somewhere.

And you should know as you sail you can go no further
than the far side of a circle. But you should know too
that the world is deep, and that no return is certain.

Of Travelling by Land

When you have ridden over the different softnesses
of squelch and splash, leaf-sludge and pine-needle, listening
to the hoofs' slither, feeling the spindly legbones jar;

when you have checked that the shadows are in their places,
and that the hazel-twigs and willow-scrub are in theirs,
and that nothing is moving without the wind's say-so;

when you have looked up at the white above the treetops
and watched it speckle with a darkness that might be rain,
and blinked to clear your eyes, and watched it speckle harder,

and seen the light eaten away from the bottom up
until the path becomes the memory of a path
and branches happen in your face at the last moment,

and heard bushes jostling in their haste to get at you
and the forest scraping a ditch for you with its claws
and the wolves clearing their throats for a night of howling;

then you must think a spark and breathe your prayers over it
till it flickers into the world, where you must nurse it,
holding it steady against the black with both your eyes,

a low star under the trees for you to ride towards,
urging it into flame. When you smell smoke, you will know
there are people here too. Let us hope they are friendly.

Of Inns

Bread fire milk candle beer soup meat wine horse oats stable
bed straw blanket man woman cloak sword staff saddle knife
ride walk sleep eat drink fight kiss make merry say prayers.

Have you come far? Yes, I have come many miles since dawn.
What is the news? There is none. I bring news. I must eat.
Will your boy take my horse? I have money. Give me bread.

Give me soup. This wine is bad. What have you put in it?
I am a pilgrim. A merchant. I am lost. Help me.
I am sick. Tired. I am wounded. I have hurt my foot.

Now I will go to bed. Where is it? Give me a light.
There is no blanket. This straw is fouled. There is no room.
A man in my bed is snoring. Singing. Go to sleep.

Good morning, fellow. Where are you from? Where do you go?
Are you a heretic? In my country we do thus.
I need food for the journey. I must ride far today.

Of Foreign Tongues

Night in a monastery, monks hiccuping in Latin.
Roomed with two Germans and a Portuguese. Too much wine.
Woke in the dark with foreign words dancing in your head.

Your own words are all spent. If the people here speak French
it is a kind of French you never heard in England.
You make the round sign for bread with your fingers and thumbs.

Rain spits soft on your cloak. A man comes tugging a cow
round a bend in the red road. There is an apple tree
with a jackdaw in it. They look and sound like themselves.

The man sounds like a man, a curse being much the same
in any language. But underneath the sound and look
the meaning of things has changed: rain road tree bird cow man

broken into pieces and floating before your eyes,
as if it was only the words that held them in place.
You are riding through an unnamed land. Something takes wing.

Of the Road

You live at a clopped walk now. The peasants in the fields
stoop to the crops as if they too were gripped by the earth
and yet as you watch them they lollop into the past.

Then there are new crops, other rooted men, a village,
a grey castle clamped on its crag, yet drifting away,
a gnarled forest of vines you ride through like a giant,

as the sun battens on you, the dust smells of sweet herbs
and you feel the word south on your tongue like a dryness,
marvelling at the strangers who breathe it all the time.

Your home now is a straggle of walkers and riders
born at a fork in the road who jog along with you
laugh, share their bread, then pass away at the next crossroads,

and you outlive them as you make your way south and east,
towards a line of mountains the same colour as air,
gilded with snow. The rest of the world is behind them,

and to reach it you must travel over the passes,
leading your horse along the rocky paths not thinking
of the fall, end over end, to a snow-cushioned death,

and stagger down, counting your burning fingers and toes,
to a valley stiff with cypresses, soft with olives.
This is the road to Venice, where the pilgrims sail from.

Of Relics

As there are metals and stones that have light inside them,
gold, silver and jewels that are polished to a shine,
which is only the leaping-out of what God locked in,

so there are spiritual shinings, a saint's thighbone,
a scrap of robe, a charred twig snapped from the Burning Bush,
things that were steeped in God like the wick of an oil-lamp

and now light up the dark of a church, sweeten its air,
that leave a glow on the lips that have kissed their casket,
on fingers that touch what so many fingers have smoothed.

At Constantinople is the sponge, now pumice-hard,
from which Our Lord was given vinegar on the Cross.
In France is a thorn from his crown, the nail from his feet.

In Cyprus at the Hill of the Holy Cross, they keep
an arm's-length of stony wood, with teethmarks where pilgrims
have nibbled bits to take home. They say Christ died on it,

but it is not so. St Dismas, the good thief, hung there.
The True Cross is of olive, palm, cypress and cedar.
It was found, but is scattered. Do not hope to see it.

But you may kneel in France and in Constantinople
before two spearheads, and know that one of them was lodged
in the body of Christ (the shaft is in Germany),

or visit the tomb where St John laid himself alive
to wait for the Day of Judgement, and watch the packed earth
that shivers sometimes as he turns over in his sleep.

You may see stone cups that drip themselves full of water,
a plaque that was dug up with an ancient corpse, inscribed
Christ will be born of a Virgin. I believe in him.

There is light in these objects, and pardon for your sins,
matter for gazing and telling, if you can find them.
Cut out these pages of my book. Carry them with you.

Of the West Sea

The time is long gone when you could have turned to the west
and joined the seekers after St James's scallop-shells.
Now you are leaving those who file to Rome for the keys,

and travelling to the Holy Land, to wear the palm,
a place that is all relic, with its white bones of hills
and the footprints of the Apostles baked into them.

You will stand in the dust that Our Lord brushed with his robe,
in the heat of a scorched country that God has passed through,
where spent miracles lie around like the husks of flies.

But first you must cross that arm of the Great Sea Ocean
that lies between Europe and Africa, the West Sea.
It is wide and deep, and spattered in winter with storms,

but, being surrounded by land, has an inwardness
as of an imagined sea, too blue to be real,
and it is strewn with islands, stepping-stones to your goal.

Of Islands

Here is an island where they make good wine; here is one
where they hunt game with leopards the way we hunt with
   hounds;
here the sun is so hot they crouch in paved pits to eat;

and here is an island infested by a woman-
dragon one hundred feet long, though I have not seen it,
the lady of the castle, bewitched by a goddess.

There was a man who left his ship to go for a walk,
came to a chamber and found a girl combing her hair.
He was behind her and glimpsed her face in the mirror.

What do you want? she asked. I want to be your lover.
I will love only a knight, she told him. Seeing her
silvered by the glass, he vowed to come back and have her,

but when he returned and she oozed out of the castle,
steaming, he looked at her fire-cracked lips, and ran away.
She followed, and swam round the ship wailing, till he died.

One good kiss would be enough to flake off those green scales
but you sail on. A new island looms – beneath the sea.
There was a city, a man who loved, a girl who died.

One night he shifted the marble slab, and unwrapped her,
and nine months later a voice spoke in his sleep: Go back
and see what you have made. Again he lifted the lid.

A feathered thing flew out with a scream, as if a bird
had been trapped inside. He saw it roosting on a branch,
the claws tight under its chin. It was a human head.

For three days it flapped over the city, a winged moon
crying revenge on him who had caused it to be born,
until the sea answered it and crashed over the walls.

Islands and stories. Every time you arrive, you think
how it would feel to pull the sea around you at night,
except that the next land floats in the distance, waiting.

Of Egypt

If you should see the Sultan's shadow at the window
of his castle, high on its rock above the city,
kneel and kiss the ground at once. You will know who he is.

And when you enter the castle and kneel before him,
do not be afraid of the men with their drawn swords raised,
ready to strike off your head, but speak respectfully,

tell him you wish to see St Catherine at Mount Sinai,
as a pilgrim should, and ask leave to cross his desert.
Mention the name of Mandeville. He will remember.

You are in Egypt, a land that clings to its river
because it never rains, and all the water it has
is spread on the ground, and rises at certain seasons,

which makes the earth so rich it bears crops eight times a year,
while the leftover green solidifies to crystal
and becomes emeralds, of which they have a glut here,

but neither the soft nor the hard green will grow elsewhere,
so the rest of the country is brown and powdery,
flounced into stinging clouds by the winds. This you must cross.

Remind him I fought for him against the Bedouin.
We have talked many times in this room till it was late
and the men grew tired and lowered their swords to the ground,

and he would have had me marry a prince's daughter
if I would give up my faith, but I did not want to.
Wear cloth of gold when you go there. Or camlet will do.

Of the Market

They set up the stalls as soon as they see you coming,
flopping crosslegged on the street under their tent-robes
offering a tray to pick from, a bin to delve in:

figs, grapes, nuts. Here is a long yellow fruit, blotched with
    brown.
The flesh is soft with a flavour of meal and honey
but you must strip it naked before you can eat it.

Other fruit dangles from the branch but these grow upwards,
raised to their green heaven like a many-fingered prayer.
They are the apples of Paradise which tempted Eve.

And if you cut one open there is a cross inside
as if inlaid in dark wood within the creaminess,
for God leaves his mark everywhere in his creation.

Your hand burns with the balm of Gilead, an ointment
that can heal wounds, dry sweat from the brow, soothe a sore
    mouth.
There are balm bush twigs in the nest where the Phoenix burns,

and you can feel the runny fire in it now. True balm
will catch light in a flame, curdle a bowl of goat's milk.
Some is eked out with turpentine or cloves, but not this.

The chickens bobbing about your feet are the offspring
of the Cairo Incubator. Women take eggs there,
lay them in wooden nests and cover them with horse dung.

And the inside of the dung is a mother to them
so that they need no flesh-and-feather one to brood them,
but are coddled by warm excrement, caked in its love.

After a short time in that richness they crack their shells
as a shoot cracks its seed, and put forth their yellow heads
till the air seethes with their chirping and the smelly steam.

In the street the camels are tethered, one hoof bent up,
chewing at nothing with their loose lips. They seem too tall
for the city. Soon they will be walking on the sand.

Of the Pyramids

Nearby in the desert there are great nipples of stone
or sculpted mountains, which some say are the tombs of kings
but which now hold only snakes and a sandy darkness.

What corpse would have been vast enough for such a
    dwelling?
When I first entered the silence of those hewn spaces
I thought instead of the Scriptures: these are Joseph's barns.

Seven harvests were entombed in them, wagons of grain
reckoned by the scribes, cats slipping in from the desert
to lie in wait for the mice that scrabbled and shat there.

The smell of musty gold lingers inside, as of corn
long ago shovelled out for the Pharaoh's bread-ovens
leaving a flitter of chaff to harden into sand.

Of the Phoenix

Only the priest of the temple knows when it was born.
He has the date in a book, so he can be ready,
when its time has come, to build the fire on the altar:

cinnamon, cloves, nutmeg, twigs of balm, virgin sulphur.
It will be heaped up, unlit, when the bird blunders in,
faffing between the pillars like a panicked sparrow,

but the size of an eagle, its colours now tarnished
by five hundred years of sandstorms. Yet it remembers
at last what to do, and climbs on to its nest of spice,

lifting its neck and fanning with its wings till the sparks
wake in the dull feathers and catch in their own tinder.
Then it is sitting on flame, and the smell fills the air,

incense, banquet and bonfire in one. Its trumpetings
are triumph seasoned with agony. When they die down
there is nothing left but a puffy cushion of ash.

Next day the priest sifts through the coolness with his fingers
and finds a maggot no bigger than a nail paring,
which, by the next, has formed into a body and wings.

And by the third morning it is a whole bird, preening
the last ash from its scarlet wings and indigo back.
It sputters once more round the tall spaces, and flies out.

There is only one in the world. If you should see it,
a dragonfly speck overhead as you cross the sand,
it is a sign of good luck. Your journey will prosper.

Of Mount Sinai

In the church of St Catherine, the monks' souls are burning,
oily flames scattered through the arched dark. The lamps are
    fuelled
by olive branches brought each year by the rooks and crows,

as if these gowned birds sensed some kinship with holy men.
When a monk dies his light goes out. When an abbot dies
the next one's name appears in a scroll on the altar.

They will show you her bones on this altar, moving them
with a silver instrument designed for the purpose
until a little oil comes out of them, like black sweat,

essence of saint. Then they will show you her dried-up head
wrapped in the cloth in which the angels carried it here,
and give you some of the oil to take on your journey.

Later, standing by the spring Moses struck from the rock,
and climbing the cold mountain where God gave him the Law,
you can feel the flask of oil next to your skin, balm-warm.

Of Bethlehem and Jerusalem

When you have used a knife or a cup and put it down,
after it comes to rest and your warmth has gone from it,
and though there is no mark of your hand on grip or bowl,

there is a moment when you still have each other's shape,
when your skin remembers it, and it remembers you,
like a part of yourself you left, and must go back for.

These are the places that God used and has just put down.
A narrow city, well-walled and moated, that he used
for being born in. There is a church built on the spot.

Here was the manger of the ox and ass. Beside it,
the place where the star of the Magi fell and went out.
You can see white drops of Our Lady's milk on these stones.

And here, in a church in Jerusalem, is Christ's tomb,
which he cast off as an insect shucks its outgrown skin.
There is a hill in the church with steps leading up it,

where the cross was. He left some of his blood beneath it.
And this circle marks the place where his body was laid:
it is the gold pin piercing the centre of the world.

Of the Temple of Jerusalem

To enter the Temple, you need leave from the Sultan,
but you have leave. Take off your shoes as Saracens do,
for this white pillared space is sacred to them also.

Walk in a whisper. This is the *Sancta Sanctorum*.
The Ark of the Covenant was here, a wooden chest
that held the Tablets of the Law, the staff of Moses,

a gold vessel of manna, seven gold candlesticks,
twelve gold phials, a gold altar with four gold lions
and gold cherubim on it, a gold tabernacle,

besides twelve silver trumpets and seven holy loaves.
It is now lost. And this is the rock where Jacob dreamt
of angels going up and down the stairs of the sky.

Of the Dead Sea

This sea has sulked so long it has forgotten wetness.
Slumped in its bed, it is too weary to raise a wave
or a few fish. There is nothing to be done with it.

It has swallowed its tears and become parched by the salt,
halfway to desert already, the water gluey.
It will seek out your eyes, or a cut, with its Greek fire.

They call it dead but it is swaddled in fevered sleep.
Sometimes it dreams itself full of blood, or remembers
what it was like to be fished and, convulsing itself,

coughs up a gob of sticky black the size of a horse.
The beach is smirched with them. Throw anything into it,
a lamp, a lump of iron, a feather, a felon,

and you only add to its confusion. It gulps down
a feather or an unlit lamp, but iron will float,
and flame floats beside it. The sea will have none of them,

and you must drown your chained man elsewhere: it spits him
    out.
Sodom was salted down here, and Lot's wife crystallised.
Now nothing grows on the shore but apples stuffed with ash.

Of the Sea of Galilee

To the north is another sea, innocent of salt,
where Christ lived as a youth, and made his first miracles
out of whatever he found to hand: water, bread, fish,

learning the distinction between nothing and something
from wind scrawling on the surface, boats casting their nets
into one silver and coming up with another.

Here he found fishermen and turned them into preachers,
and on these waters he slept in the boat while they fished
and woke rubbing the storm from the sky like a blurred dream.

Once, late for the boat, he went to meet it, forgetting
the only way was water, and set foot on the waves
to find they would take his weight. When they saw him coming,

a man on the sea in the half-and-half light of dawn,
they knew part of it was not real, and guessed the man,
as if they had not yet grasped how things changed around him.

Then Peter got out to join him, keeping his mind fixed
on the slipperiness underfoot, to hold it down
as a drunk man stops the ground from rising beneath him,

with one hand stretching for his Lord's and one on the air,
and had almost reached him when his mind lost its footing.
Afterwards they huddled in the boat, one drenched, one dry,

and the world in its place again, sea, shoreline, weather,
as you will find it, who have seen much water thus far
and eaten your share of fish. They catch some fine ones here.

Of the Assassins

You may travel these mountain paths and fear little more
than the teeth of beasts, of snowstorms, of the rocks below –
what bandits there are will only kill you for money.

For the old man of the mountains is dead. His castle
is a crown of stones, the trees in the garden ramble,
the streams that flowed with wine, honey and milk are dry
    smears.

There were nightingales once, and women who could match
    them
note for note. There were flutes and zithers playing all night
in a high tower so that it sounded like angels.

Walls kept the wind out. The smell of jasmine oiled the dark,
and there were woven summerhouses to shelter in
where girls waited to tend to men in the candlelight.

He had mechanics and gardeners to build this place,
and a herb he would give to the young men in a drink
that poisoned time and made a caress last forever.

This garden was their paradise. They left it in tears,
and stumbled on to the icy passes, grasping knives
to cut their way back with. They would die to return there.

Viziers, caliphs, nizams were killed in their ambushes,
their litters capsized, their guards thrown over the edge.
These men kept stabbing as the blood ran from their death-
    wounds.

But you need not fear them. The Old Man of the Mountains
is gone, and his paradise is shattered. The bandits
who lurk here now are as frightened as you, and mortal.

Of the Land of Darkness

From this height it is a leggy black shape, a crushed fly
between the greens and blues. The sun does not glance off it,
or pass inside. It is not a blotch on your eyeball.

As you descend you lose sight of it, but you still feel
a pressure behind the horizon, like a headache.
You question the people you meet in the marketplace.

The land is called Hamschen. It has not always been dark.
There were Christians living there once, but the Emperor
forced them to worship his gods, so they gathered in tents,

an army without weapons preparing to escape,
and when the pagan soldiers marched on their soft city,
they prayed to God, who fell on the foe with his blackness.

Now if you pass through the penumbra near the border,
you may hear the sound of voices, the neigh of a horse,
a cock spluttering for a dawn that will never break

as if behind a wall. Nobody knows who lives there,
but there is a river that flows through carrying proof
that they are people like us, and have the same workings.

Of the Amazons

They fly back across the water like birds to their nests,
fording the river on their great horses, or on foot.
They reach the township and fall on their husbands with cries.

Then there is whispering and laughter, the relearning
of textures and smells. After the bodily pleasures
each lies awake, with a round pain where one breast should be.

They bring toys for their sons, but not wooden swords or
     knights,
and the boys peer round their fathers' legs at these women
who carry a smile more hesitantly than a bow.

This is less real to them than campfires and trumpets.
Their bodies warm slowly to gentleness. They expect
cold, shouting and fear. The shape of a man means danger.

Yet here are men kicking stones in the street, gossiping
in voices like bulls, or crows. There are old and fat ones,
unfinished ones with scattered hairs on their upper lips

who will be at a loose end for the rest of their lives.
They make the women feel guilty, as if these beings
were a task they had meant to get round to and forgot.

But they must leave it now and go back to their daughters
fighting with sticks among the tents. Soon it will be time
for these to go under the knife and be made single.

Of Being Lost

After the ridge, another ridge. After the kingdom,
another valley kingdom for you to climb down to,
a mizmaze of farms, a village under its damp smoke.

You have seen the market, stood in the way of the rain
while gutturals were hawked in your ear. You have gestured:
Where am I? Which is the way . . . ? Have I been here before?

At least you can climb out. I have heard of a valley
so wedged in behind its escarpments and overhangs
that no one can enter or leave. The lost tribe lives there,

scratching the tally of days on the rock till at last
a fox will find them, burrowing in from the outside.
They will follow its red through the darkness and be free.

You stand on another ridge. The far-off green dissolves
into a glare of white. You hate the words Inland Sea –
it is a distance that goes nowhere, like a mirror.

You have no wish to drown without leaving the mountains.
You are going to India. You will find some fox,
and work back to the Great Sea Ocean, where you can
    breathe.

Of Rocks that Enchant Ships

Few merchants visit India. The sea is guarded
by rocks of adamant whose lust for iron is such
that they will draw the nails of a passing ship to them,

I have seen an island so furred with bushes and trees
that none could set foot there. Beneath the thickets, the hulls
of a hundred ships were barnacled, held by the nails.

The grain and fruit in the holds had sprouted through the planks
and made off, like outlaws, into their own wilderness,
which we sailed by, for the nails in our ship were of wood.

Of Pepper

This is the forest where all the world's pepper comes from,
and you could believe fire grows here, as you tug your horse
through the green snarl of animal and vegetable,

creepers and suckers, in the cloaked heat. Everything bites,
or strangles, or flies away, or gives birth underfoot.
Here the three kinds of pepper grow, draped from the tree-
     trunks,

the long pepper, like catkins, which comes before the leaves,
then the white berries clustered among the leaves like grapes,
and, last, the black, which is toasted, or dried in the sun –

all three on one vine infested with poisonous snakes,
and those who woud pick them must rub their hands with the
     juice
of a fruit called lemons, which the snakes are afraid of.

These puckered pellets of spice that you carry away
are more potent than money. Some merchants water them
with frothy matter of silver to make up the weight.

A strange coinage, that you can take in your mouth and chew.
There is no silver in these. They come straight from the vine.
You can taste the sun and the snakes and the stinging fruit.

Of Diamonds

There are many Indias. This one is hard and cold.
Water freezes to ice, and ice becomes petrified
to crystal. On the rocks of crystal, diamonds grow,

feeding on frost and the scant sunlight, male and female
engendering smaller diamonds after their kind.
If you pull one up by the roots, with some of its bed,

keep it and water it, it grows a little each year,
brooding on its colours like a dragon on its hoard,
or spitting them into the air in Platonic sparks.

Beware of lesser stones in disguise. If offered one,
test with a magnet and needle – it should kill their love.
When poison is nearby, it grows cold and starts to sweat.

Wear a diamond on the left side of your body
and no vicious or venomous creature will harm you.
It protects against lunacy, witchcraft and nightmares.

But if you misbehave it shrinks back into a rock
until a worthier owner comes to cosset it.
You must live up to it. Its morals are mineral.

Of Ants that Dig for Gold

You have seen ants in the grass, held one on your finger.
You have watched them weave and unweave their tickling
    footsteps,
study their path with their horns, or manhandle a seed.

And you were pleased with the fiddliness of their concerns,
the fumbled meetings and stalk-clinging. It seemed to you
like a smallness of your own you had stepped away from.

But this is a place where the ants are as big as dogs,
and yet like those you know they are busy with the earth,
which is of gold here, loose hills of it mingled with dirt.

All day long they crawl over the scree, worrying out
the nuggets and letting them roll away down the slope,
then gathering them into scabby heaps of glitter.

Who knows what they want with gold? They will fight to keep
    it,
and everyone is afraid of their pincering jaws,
so if you want to enrich yourself you must trick them,

using a mare and two clay pots, hung so she drags them
with their mouths clunking along the ground towards the ants,
which cannot see a hole without putting gold in it.

Then lead her foal as close as you dare to call her back
with her two pots behind her, shaking out raw money,
the earth's shiny droppings. Is this what you are after?

Of the Animals of India

The crocodile is a snake, with legs that just suffice
to raise its horny bulk off the ground. Where it has passed
the sand is scuffed as if someone has dragged a tree there.

So weary is it from heaving the belly God pressed
in the dust that it may pass a winter without food.
It stretches its body on the rocks and becomes them,

then lies in the water up to its eyes and nostrils,
or forgets to finish a yawn, so that a small bird
may enter the tongueless gulch of the mouth without harm,

and you may see it stepping there, in a cave of teeth,
winkling out in-betweens under the lean of a jaw
that would twist the leg off you as you tear a chicken.

But there is another snake that forgets God's command
and stands, like a beast on a shield. It has a cock's crest
and its mouth is always open, to spit its poison.

Fear it as you go through the high passes. In the plains
fear the rhinoceros with three sharp swords on its brow.
I have often seen it chase and kill an elephant.

And there are lizards that change colour as we change clothes,
and wild pigs the size of oxen, and a dappled horse
whose neck is stretched so long he could see over a house.

As you wake from one India into another,
the dream-animals shimmer and swim into new shapes.
Yet they are real. God made them. They must mean something.

Of Prester John

Prester John is Emperor here, who has three crosses
of gold borne tottering before him into battle,
to smite his enemies with the light of their jewels,

who rides in time of peace after a cross of plain wood
and a gold dish laden with dirt as a reminder
of the loam beneath that we grow from and die back to

and the ores that gleam there, whose palace is illumined
at night by the glow of carbuncles on the towers,
whose windows are crystal, whose tables are emerald,

who sways in his ermine to the throne up seven steps
of onyx, crystal, jasper, amethyst, sardonyx,
coral and chrysolite, who sleeps in a sapphire bed

in the syrupy smoke from twelve braziers of balm,
who has as many wives as a sultan, lies with them
only on quarter days for the getting of children,

who has seven kings to serve him, seventy-two dukes,
three hundred and sixty earls, dines with twelve archbishops
and twenty bishops and thirty thousand courtiers,

whose land is four months' ride from one end to the other,
as I can attest, having ridden every furlong
when I was in his service and lived in the palace,

whose land holds parrots that speak with the voices of men,
hazelnuts as big as your head, hairy men with horns,
and a fruit that grows all day and withers at sunset,

who prays to the Father, the Son and the Holy Ghost,
whose faith was planted by St Thomas and grew strange leaves,
who is John, son of John, son of John, whose name means
   Priest.

Of the Gravelly Sea

I have followed the clack and rattle of that river
that holds, not water, but a torrent of precious stones,
all bed and surface-sparkle with nothing between them.

It would have been death to wade into that grinding flood
as many have done, seeking wealth. I kept my distance,
and grew to find the noise companionable at night.

And then one evening I came to the Gravelly Sea.
It was low tide and the dry waves were like the ripples
you see carved into the unmoving sand of a shore,

except that they moved, drawn and redrawn on the stillness
as if a field could plough itself, or the desert frown.
I made my fire on the beach, far from these goings-on,

but woke to find the powder breaking over my feet.
The sea was rougher now, the waves high as a man's knee,
restless dunes that crumbled as they ran, spraying dust-spume,

and foundered with the quiet huffing of sand on sand.
There were no ships in the brown distance, for their timbers
would have been polished to nothing, and the crew smothered,

but I saw fishermen on the beach casting their nets
for there are sightless fish in that dark, just as you find
fish living buried in the sludge under our waters.

I have cooked those fish at my fire, picked out the glass bones.
(Sometimes you can find a swallowed gem from the river.)
They were tough but worth eating. Try them if you go there.

Of the Vale Perilous

After much hardship I came to the Vale Perilous
and stood on the edge, where the ground cut away, sweeping
some four miles, between craggy hills rubbled with gemstones.

Sometimes they snagged on the sunlight and drew out of it
a thread of green or blue or ruby that twisted there
only a moment before the whiteness covered it,

which was not the white of clean mist that comes from the air,
but an earth vapour that reached me and caught in my throat,
the smell of the rocky innards digesting themselves.

I did not feel the silence that goes with distances
but noises came and went, like the trundling of a storm,
or the trumpets and drums that accompany a feast.

This valley is full of devils and always has been,
yet people are drawn by the ingots lying around
and the pickings of still-warm diamonds in the scree.

But few who enter come out again, for the devils
will strangle people who go there out of avarice.
Even good Christians are afraid of their flickerings.

Some of us left to take the long way round. The rest knelt
with the priest, going over our sins behind closed eyes.
Then, with God's bread and wine glowing inside, we set off,

fourteen of us, leading our mounts down the scruffy path,
and yet as soon as the rim of the valley was lost
behind a boulder at a sharp turn I was alone

with my yard of path that the mist cleared in front of me
and my shadow gone soft, splitting and wheeling round me,
then shrinking to my feet and slipping back into me.

And sometimes a stone came pittering down like a word,
or a sentence from one of our party drifted back
translated into a coughing Dutch by the weather.

Then I came to the flat land where a river gargled
and spat on the rock. It was the colour of water
but I shrank from its spittle, drawing my horse away.

Now it was rough going over the stony surface
with a groundswell of thunder rising beneath my feet
and the jitter of lightning always in the background.

And sometimes the steam undraped itself from some stone-heap,
revealing armfuls of trinkets on their cinder bed
that sparkled to themselves in the half-hearted sunlight,

their earth mingled with fire in varying proportions
so that what seemed solid was little more than a flame
and burned as a flame does, with insubstantial colours.

There was gold also, in malformed lumps, as if the smith
had forgotten what he was doing when he forged them,
and piles of crude silver, untarnished by the vapour.

I will not deny that I was tempted: not to own
but to finger some of the treasure, or to take it
as a keepsake, or to spend in some deed of honour,

but whenever I approached a vent sputtered at me,
the clinker shuffled, the flying devils grew spiteful,
and crackled and lit the air, so that I ran away.

Then I found my first man. He lay face down, one knee up,
so that I thought at first he was crawling, and indeed
his cloak shook as if the body beneath it still moved,

and I went up to him and started to say something
but felt the wrongness of it in his unmoving head
and silence. I knew then that the soul had gone from him,

but without tearing the body, which I dared not touch
for fear of disturbing its long study of the ground.
He held a leather bag of sapphires in his left hand.

After that I grew accustomed to the dead, which lazed
unrotting all around me, their limbs bent forever
into the ragged capitals of their last gestures.

Eventually I reached the outcrop in the middle
where the lightning swarmed and the smoke was at its thickest.
Here the chief devil was buried up to the shoulders,

that battlement of rock holding him down, so only
his eyes could move behind their glaze of quartz, and the flame
and fumes of his tongue. He changed colour a dozen times,

and cursed in his igneous language. I could not pass
but trembled and crossed myself and repeated my prayers
like a traveller searching for an overgrown path

or someone who batters his knuckles against a door,
knowing the street is watching him, and hearing only
silence behind it, or the creak of the house stretching.

Then gorse, brambles and bracken let go and fall away,
the door swings open before your knock. This way forward
is granted to you, John Mandeville, as you have asked.

And now my feet could move I looked again at the face
and found it had stopped scowling and vanished into rock.
A little flame moved, sad at having nothing to burn.

Fourteen of us entered that valley, leading our mounts
down the scruffy path. One at a time, leading our mounts
up the hill at the far end we climbed out of the mist,

singing, hailing our friends, saying a left-over prayer.
We looked at each other. None had a bulkier pack
than he had entered with, and there were nine of us now.

I cannot say if the dead men I saw were real.
Those jewels may have been illusions. I know only
that never before or since have I been so devout.

Of the Ceremonies of the Great Khan

One has an astrolabe, one the scalp of a dead man,
one gazes into glowing coals, another studies
the coiling blobs of a bowl of water, wine and oil.

These are the Great Khan's men of learning: astronomers,
necromancers, pyromancers, and hydromancers,
men who trap time in clocks, or see through it in crystals.

One says, Bow! And the courtiers bump heads with the earth.
A second says, Put your little fingers in your ears!
A third, Put your hands in front of your mouths! And they do,

four thousand emirs in the heavy air of a tent,
each with his table in front of him, and the women
in foot-shaped head-dresses of gold and peacock feathers.

Nine white horses, a leopard, a mechanical bird
riffling its filigree plumage on the tabletop –
no one must come before the Great Khan without a gift.

Then the magicians enter, bringing the sun and moon
that swim through the tent burning with unlookable light.
Even these bob their bodiless heads to the Great Khan.

It is dark, then day again. A girl stands in the air
offering a cup of mare's milk that a blink dissolves.
Knights clash. Spear-splinters fall on the dishes and are gone.

Then in the shadowy woodland under the tables,
there is the gibbering of a boar, the skirl of hounds
who hunt him through the ins and outs, tear him to nothing

before the Great Khan, who swallows the last of his meal
but does not wipe his hands Tartar fashion on his clothes –
it is not seemly for the Emperor of Cathay.

He orders all these appearances and vanishings,
for he stands with his foot on the head of the world. Bow!
Block ears, cover your mouth, in case a whisper creeps through.

Of the Tartars

When one of these men is dying, his friends stab his spear
into the earth floor, and leave him in the tent of sticks
he lived in, letting the felt door flop down behind them.

He has taken this house to war with him on a cart.
His life weighed as little as the smoke that breathes out through
the chimney-window, and it leaves him now the same way.

By this fire he has eaten the meat of dogs and rats,
horses and lions, and wiped the grease from his fingers,
making himself tipsy on the sour froth of mare's milk.

He will die alone, who had thirty or forty wives
to wear the wiry shape of his foot as a head-dress,
and visited them in their huts to have dalliance,

women who could shoot with a bow as straight as he could,
and run without a sound in their loose shirts and breeches,
drive a plough or a wagon, put together a hut.

In his silk undershirt, his breastplate of boiled leather,
with three bows and a battle-axe, he was to be feared
riding away, for he could turn right round like an owl.

No one could trust his promises. He has killed many
and cut off their ears to be pickled in vinegar
and served to the lords after the town has been taken.

He believed in one God who made all things, and offered
the first milk of his animals, the first lump of meat
to the idols of felt and cloth he carried with him.

A man with small eyes and a scrap of beard, one of those
who rode with the Great Khan over the plains of Asia,
and I rode among them against the King of Manzi.

Now the hut is cooling and he lies in the smoke haze
as his friends return to take him out and bury him
in the flat green that is their idea of forever.

Of the Vegetable Lamb

It will not do to look for it if you are hungry.
It grows among rocks, in places where the only plants
are flakes of yellowish grey and skeins of brown crackle,

where the stream, if there is one, finds no soil to moisten
but fidgets a few yards then slips back into the ground.
Swallow a handful and it tastes of rusty armour.

You can search this hardness a long time and not find it,
then trip over it when you stop to relieve yourself:
an ankle-trap of knitted stems baited with one fruit.

It takes a knife to split the rind, but the pith inside,
woolly as you would expect, is sweet and chewable.
In the hollow heart the lamb stretches and looks at you.

It will die anyway now you have opened its womb,
and besides, what kind of a life did it have in there?
No more than an egg. It could do nothing but nestle.

It would have hatched into daylight and scrambled away
to some new cranny where its legs would twist into roots,
its eyes atrophy, the raw skin toughen to fibre.

One twist of your knife is enough: the cocoon reddens.
You quarry the meat from the bones. It is like liver
scented with honey. You would not want too much of it.

Of Apes Said to Contain Human Souls

Some of the trees held out an offering of flowers.
Their robes of leaves did not move. Like the monk beneath
    them
they found a repose in standing. When he rang the bell,

it seemed to me less a sound than a change in the air
to the chill metal of the river I arrived by,
yet something came of it, a stirring between the roots.

There was a village down there, of apes and marmosets
that clambered up now and ran to him over the grass
jostling to get at the rice and fruit he had brought them.

Each of these long-armed beasts has the soul of a human,
the monk said. They were virtuous in their former lives
to receive such forms. They might have been toads or bedbugs.

I knew he was wrong, but seeing a butterfly pass,
I imagined myself trapped in its feelers and wings
before one of the apes tore it to powdery shreds.

The rice they scattered about them was meant for the poor,
but the monk insisted there were no poor in Cathay,
only those who had fallen to lowness, and must crawl.

Of Island Peoples

Beyond Cathay the world peters out into islands.
You have grown used to the craziness of such places,
the way they hide in the sea to nurse their delusions.

Here are the one-eyed giants who eat raw flesh and fish,
here the people with no heads and eyes in each shoulder,
whose mouths are like horseshoes in the middle of their chests.

And here the faces are flat, without noses or eyes,
just two small holes to see through and a slit of a mouth.
Here they can stretch their lips to shield their brows from the sun.

And these dwarfs have a pipe instead of a mouth. To speak
they must hiss and make signs to each other, as monks do.
In this island the people's ears hang down to their knees.

So much for the faces. Here are some people with hoofs
galloping after a deer. And these walk on all fours
and are furry, and can climb trees as well as an ape.

A man lies on his back in the shade of his one foot,
as broad as that of an oak. He can bound like a frog.
Others run on their knees, half-toppling at every step.

And here they live on the smell of a kind of apple –
if it is taken away they die. I have tried it,
that sumptuous smell, and I was not hungry for days.

But when you reach the land of the hermaphrodites, where
out-in, hard-tender, hairy-smooth meet on one body,
you dare not look at them. Is the whole world dissolving?

Of a Manner of Disposing of the Dead

Here is an island where they leave the dead for the birds.
Eagles, vultures and ravens fall on them from the air
while the priests sing the *Subvenite, Sancti Dei*

of those regions, and when they fly off there is nothing
the kin knew on the ground. They boast of how many came:
My father was honoured by twenty, or thirty, birds.

These people think birds are angels. When some pass over
they say: My father is flying with them, scattering
here and there round the island. You can hear him calling.

Of Paradise

The last land you reach is a desert. No one can cross
because of its snakes and tigers, its crags and darkness.
There is a river that is too rapid to sail up,

too loud for travellers to hear each other shouting.
Paradise lies beyond, the highest place in the world,
almost touching the moon. There is a wall around it

so thick with moss and bushes the stone cannot be seen.
The gate is made of fire – this is the sword and angel
God set there to keep us out. Inside is the garden

of Adam and Eve, the snake and the Tree of Knowledge.
A spring rises in the centre and flows out to form
four rivers: the Ganges, Nile, Tigris and Euphrates.

This is all I can tell you. I have never been there,
which I regret, for it is said to be beautiful.
We must sail on. We are almost at the beginning.

Mandeville's Farewell

I, Sir John Mandeville of St Albans in England,
left my home and crossed the sea thirty-four years ago
on Michaelmas Day of the year 1332.

I have seen many countries I have not described here
for there is too much of the world to tell all of it.
I have left some for you to discover on your own.

Once I had three sips of water from the Well of Youth.
It tasted spicy and slightly sweet. Those who live near
and drink of it often never fall ill or grow old.

I felt the stronger for it, but the taste has faded,
and I am worn by travel and age and feebleness,
so I have come back to our islands on the world's edge,

and written this book. In exchange I ask for your prayers,
your words for mine. Send them out on their travels, trusting
they will find me wherever I am, as mine found you.

I, Sir John Mandeville, have travelled to here and here,
seen this wonder and that, and returned home. Believe me.
What I have said is true, or as good as, or was once.

Of Circumnavigation

I have heard of a man who left our shores and set sail
for France, then crossed the Alps to Venice, where he took ship
past the islands of the West Sea to the Holy Land.

He was lost in the mountains, found the Great Sea Ocean
and the many Indias, one after another,
and afterwards journeyed to Tartary and Cathay,

and islands whose people were melted into strangeness.
He sailed past the fringes of Paradise, and arrived
at a grey country where a man was ploughing a field.

He thought he had been there before, or somewhere like it:
the smell of rainy wind, the man's bow-legged trudging
as he turned the clods hoping to scrape up a summer.

What do you call this, fellow? Ox. What is this? A plough.
Earth water sky clouds field hill house farm village church man.
They were the same words with a different heft on the tongue.

He turned to his companions. We have almost reached home.
Over that hill we may find a road to take us there.
But his friends stayed clumped together under the drizzle.

We have travelled across the world and received only
sores, blisters, fever, wounds, chills, sunburn, hunger and thirst.
We are tired. And this may be some spell or delusion.

So the man and his friends sailed back where they had come from.
Yet I believe they might have gone a few miles further
and arrived home. For you must know that the world is round.

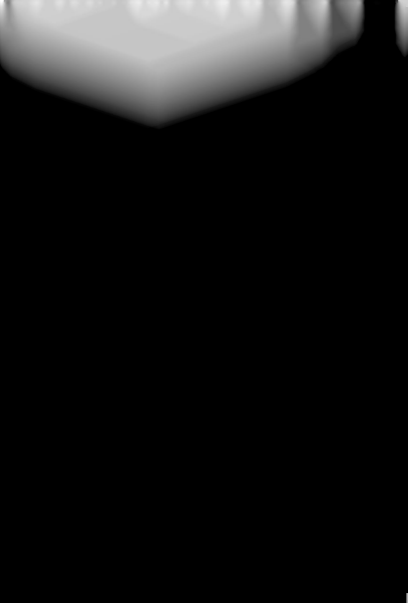

Original text by Renata Rubnikowicz
Verified by Mark Baker

© AA Media Limited 2009

ISBN: 978-0-7495-6133-8

Published by AA Publishing, a trading name of AA Media Limited, whose registered
office is Fanum House, Basing View, Basingstoke, Hampshire RG21 4EA. Registered
number 06112600.

Colour separation: MRM Graphics Ltd
Printed and bound in Italy by Printer Trento S.r.l.

A03607
Maps in this title produced from map data supplied by Global Mapping, Brackley, UK
Copyright © Global Mapping/Daunpol
Transport map © Communicarta Ltd, UK

About this book

Symbols are used to denote the following categories:

➕ map reference to maps on cover

✉ address or location

☎ telephone number

🕐 opening times

👆 admission charge

🍴 restaurant or café on premises or nearby

Ⓜ nearest underground train station

🚌 nearest bus/tram route

🚉 nearest overground train station

⛴ nearest ferry stop

✈ nearest airport

❓ other practical information

ℹ tourist information office

➤ indicates the page where you will find a fuller description

This book is divided into six sections.

The essence of Krakow pages 6–19
Introduction; Features; Food and drink; Short break including the 10 Essentials

Planning pages 20–33
Before you go; Getting there; Getting around; Being there

Best places to see pages 34–55
The unmissable highlights of any visit to Krakow

Best things to do pages 56–69
Top activities, best churches, best museums and more

Exploring pages 70–139
The best places to visit in Krakow, organized by area

Excursions pages 140–151
Places to visit out of town

Maps
All map references are to the maps on the covers. For example, Dom Śląski has the reference ➕ 6B – indicating the grid square in which it is to be found

Admission prices
Inexpensive: under 13PLN
Moderate: 13–23PLN
Expensive: over 23PLN

Hotel prices
Prices are per room per night:
€ inexpensive (under 250PLN)
€€ moderate (250–500PLN)
€€€ expensive to luxury (over 500PLN)

Restaurant prices
Price for a three-course meal for one person, without drinks:
€ under 100PLN
€€ 100–170PLN
€€€ over 170PLN

Contents

The essence of...

Although the street plan of Krakow's Old Town has not changed since it was laid out in the 13th century, and the city numbers more than 100 churches among its beautifully restored historic buildings, it's anything but frozen in time. Its many students keep this university city young and innovative, so there are also more than 400 clubs and bars, often squeezed into the cellars of grand houses once owned by medieval noble families. The castle and cathedral on Wawel Hill, signs that this was once capital of Poland, look down on the lively scene, while the former Jewish district of Kazimierz beyond is being revived, its synagogues restored and its cafés busy once more.

Do you like looking at baroque architecture or sampling new beers or vodka flavours in cosy bars? In Krakow you can do both, and much more. In the Old Town you'll find a restaurant that first opened its doors in 1364, and the tradition of hospitality continues. Many bars and clubs stay open until the last guest finally decides to call it a night.

If you are more of a lark than an owl and keen on culture, you'll find Krakow's rich history has left it with a wealth of treasures, today mainly found in churches and museums, despite the many wars and troubles the city has suffered since it became capital of Poland in around 1038. For a couple of centuries, Poland effectively ceased to exist, partitioned between neighbouring powers. And in the 20th century, some of the worst atrocities of World War II took place near here, at Auschwitz, though the buildings survived unscathed.

More recently, under Soviet domination, the Old Town's buildings were threatened by pollution from the vast industrial complexes of the new suburb of Nowa Huta. This menace has now

receded, the country's economy is flourishing again, and the renovation work continues on the stucco facades of the town houses and the old stone and brick of the churches. Through all this, the strong Polish desire for independence has asserted itself time and again. Krakow is where many insurrections and rebellions against outside rule began and even when political autonomy was not possible, the people maintained personal independence, keeping up the strong creative traditions of painting, sculpture, music,

theatre and cinema and showing Polish spirit by mocking their rulers in satirical cabaret. The first Polish Pope, John Paul II (Karol Wojtyła), who was Bishop of Krakow and once a Krakow student, became a focus and symbol of Poland's renewal.

LOCATION

Situated in southwest Poland about 100km (62 miles) from the Tatra Mountains, which straddle the border with the Czech Republic and Slovakia, Krakow began as a crossroads on ancient trade routes between Western Europe and Asia and between the Baltic and the Mediterranean. It has always been a cosmopolitan city, welcoming merchants bringing silk from the East and amber from the north.

POPULATION

About three-quarters of a million people live in Krakow. It is a young city: 60 per cent are under the age of 45. Many come to study. The oldest and most celebrated place of learning is the Jagiellonian University, whose predecessor, the Krakow Academy, was founded by King Kazimierz the Great in 1364, but there are many other universities and colleges.

THE ESSENCE OF KRAKOW

Polish food is not all about dumplings, potatoes and sausages washed down with vodka, although it is true that in certain Krakow restaurants specializing in traditional food and rustic decor, you will be given a little pot of lard studded with tasty pork morsels in which to dip your bread while studying the menu.

POLISH

Krakow is full of good restaurants, serving a variety of international cuisines, although the majority specialize in Polish food, which these days is being reinvented in a lighter style.

The best Polish restaurants celebrate the excellence of the available ingredients. Polish shoppers look for really tasty meat, fish, fruit and vegetables organically farmed, which is good news for restaurant chefs and diners. In fact, when Poland joined the European Union in 2004, some farmers feared they would be forced to lower the quality of their produce or use less natural methods of farming.

If you want to sample the best of Polish cooking, try one of the many restaurants specializing in wild produce – game and particularly mushrooms. Krakow's chefs are giving traditional dishes a gourmet spin. If you don't eat meat, don't despair. There are a few establishments where you can find something traditional but vegetarian that will be a bit more interesting than cheese salad.

INTERNATIONAL

Krakow has a wide range of restaurants and can offer Chinese, Indian, Mexican and Brazilian eateries. If you want a change from Polish dishes, you could try one of the Georgian, Galician, Hungarian or Ukrainian restaurants – their cuisines are related to, but different from, Poland's and are less common outside Eastern Europe. Italian is, however, the most popular international cuisine.

BUDGET EATING

This is where dumplings, *pierogi* (like little ravioli), *gołąbki* (literally 'pigeons', but actually meat and rice cooked in a cabbage leaf), and *naleśniki* (pancakes) come into their own. These are usually found in self-service restaurants. Look also for signs saying *bar mleczny*. These are canteen-style places left over from Soviet times. Prices are low and the turnover is fast, so your food will be fresh and hot. A recent innovation is the modern, self-service salad bar, where you help yourself then pay according to how much your plate weighs. Prices are clearly marked and there are usually some hot dishes on offer.

CAFÉ CULTURE

This is a wonderful city for original cafés and bars. Thankfully, the full force of the global chain coffee shop doesn't seem to have hit Krakow yet. With nearly all bars and many restaurants charging more or less the same for a beer (about 5–6PLN), your choice will often come down to music and decor. Is it to be lace tablecoths, dark wood and knick-knacks? Hawaiian plastic flowers and surfboards or a medieval cellar with pool tables? Everyone has their own preference.

It's impossible to group cake shops, cafés, bars and pubs into categories. Some cake shops will also serve other snacks and sandwiches. Some cafés will only serve tea, coffee and their home-cooked cheesecake; others serve wine and beer but not

vodka, and have a more extensive menu of snacks. Nearly all bars will have some kind of sandwich or other snack to help line your stomach, while some of the more atmospheric cellar bars have restaurant areas.

STREET FOOD

Every street in Krakow's Old Town seems to have a stall or two selling *obwarzanki* – surprisingly tasty pretzels sprinkled with poppy seeds or sesame seeds, and ideal to nibble with a beer. You'll also see the vendors of *oscypek*, with baskets of this squeaky, usually smoked, sheeps' milk cheese, traditionally made in the Tatra mountains. In winter it's grilled over braziers and sold hot in the Christmas market.

DRINKI

Yes, it is a Polish word. Another Polish word you probably know is vodka. Add *piwo* (beer) to your vocabulary and you're all set for a night on the town. Learning about vodka can be an entertainment in itself, and barstaff will be happy to teach you, though Polish vodka tends to be 80 proof, 40 per cent alcohol, so take care. Usually distilled from rye, Polish vodka also comes in various flavours, but until you see a Krakow bar you may not have appreciated quite how many. *Żubrówka*, or bison-grass vodka, and cherry-flavoured *Wiśniówka* are two of the most common. *Wyborowa*, which means exquisite, is a good brand.

Not as strong as vodka is *miód pitny*, a kind of mead drunk hot in winter. More winter warmers are *miód pitny z godżikami* (hot mead with cloves), *grzaniec galicyjski z migdałami* (hot sweet wine with almonds) and *piwo grzane* (heated beer with sweet syrup) – *imbirowym* (ginger), *malinowym* (raspberry), or *wiśniowym* (cherry). In summer, you can ask for a cold beer with one of these flavours added.

THE ESSENCE OF KRAKOW

short break

If you only have a short time to visit Krakow and would like to take home some unforgettable memories, the following suggestions will give you a wide range of sights and experiences that won't take very long, won't cost very much and will make your visit very special.

● **Walk around the Rynek Główny** (➤ 98), then try one of its cafés. The main market square is at the heart of Krakow life – for locals as well as visitors.

● **Meet one of the most popular women in Krakow** – the *Lady with an Ermine*. Painted by Leonardo da Vinci, she hangs in the Czartoryski Museum (➤ 44).

● **Trace the Royal Route** that the kings of Poland took on their way to be crowned, from the Barbican (➤ 74) and Florian's Gate

(► 74–75) towards Wawel Hill. Now it's lined with smart shops, as well as historic buildings.

● **Rest your feet before dinner** while listening to some uplifting classical music – perhaps in one of Krakow's beautiful churches. SS Peter and Paul on ul. Grodzka (► 83) has regular concerts.

● **Spend an hour or two** in one of the Old Town's atmospheric cellar bars – you'll be drinking in the 13th century.

● **Brave the dragon's lair** (► 50–51). You can climb down into the cave of the legendary beast from the top of Wawel Hill or meet its fiery breath face-on at the river entrance.

● **Search for souvenirs in the Sukiennice** (► 54–55). Always the main trading place of the city, the old Cloth Hall has adapted to selling amber, leather goods and wooden boxes.

● **Visit the cathedral on Wawel Hill** (► 40–41). It holds the tombs of the kings and queens of Poland – and you'll find some of its poets and heroes in the crypt. Make sure your love life goes well by putting your hand on the great Zygmunt bell that hangs above Wawel Cathedral.

● **Don't forget Kazimierz.**
Though it is fast being restored and rebuilt, and new cafés, clubs and restaurants are opening all the time here, on ul. Szeroka (➤ 123) you can still feel the atmosphere of a vanished past, when this area was home to one of the most thriving Jewish communities in Europe.

● **Go to college** – the Jagiellonian University to be precise. Arrive at the right time and you will hear its musical clock play the university song and see its carved figures move around the dial (➤ 36).

Planning

Before you go

WHEN TO GO

JAN	FEB	MAR	APR	MAY	JUN	JUL	AUG	SEP	OCT	NOV	DEC
1°C	3°C	8°C	14°C	19°C	22°C	23°C	23°C	19°C	13°C	6°C	2°C
33°F	37°F	46°F	56°F	67°F	71°F	74°F	74°F	65°F	56°F	43°F	36°F

High season   Low season

These are the average daily temperatures for each month. May and June are the best times to visit the city – the summer has really begun, but it is not too hot to enjoy the many festivals and the outdoor events associated with them. In summer it can be very hot, the city is extremely busy and thunderstorms can bring rain. July and August are the warmest months, but even in summer you might feel a little cold out of the sunshine.

Going into autumn, September and October can bring golden days with crisp, clear sunny weather, but nights will feel chilly by contrast. Winter can mean dank, murky, very short days, but sometimes there is snow, bringing extra atmosphere to December's Christmas market. The spring months of March and April are the most variable of all.

WHAT YOU NEED

● Required
○ Suggested
▲ Not required

Ensure your passport is stamped on arrival. A missing stamp can cause problems with Passport Control on your departure.

	UK	Germany	USA	Netherlands	Spain
Passport (valid for 6 months)	●	●	●	●	●
Visa (regulations can change – check before journey)	▲	▲	▲	▲	▲
Evidence of financial means to cover stay and departure, which includes onward or return ticket and medical and travel insurance	●	●	●	●	●
Health inoculations (tetanus and polio)	▲	▲	▲	▲	▲
Health documentation (► 23, Health Insurance)	▲	▲	▲	▲	▲
Travel insurance	○	○	○	○	○
Driving licence (national)	●	●	●	●	●
Car insurance certificate	●	●	●	●	●
Car registration document	●	●	●	●	●

WEBSITES

www.krakow.pl
www.krakow-info.com
www.cracow-life.com
www.culture.pl
www.muzeum.krakow.pl

www.karnet.krakow.pl
www.mhk.pl
www.poland.gov.pl
www.poland.travel
www.biurofestiwalowe.pl

TOURIST OFFICES AT HOME

In the UK

Polish National Tourist Office
Westgate House
Westgate
London W5 1YY
☎ 08700 675010
www.poland.travel

In the USA

Polish National Tourist Office
5 Marine View Plaza
Suite 208,
Hoboken, NJ-07030-5722,
☎ 201 420 9910
www.poland.travel

HEALTH INSURANCE

Although EU citizens can use a European Health Insurance Card (EHIC) in an emergency to receive medical or dental treatment, you should not rely on this alone. Whichever country you come from, you should consider buying travel insurance that will give you sufficient medical and emergency cover.

Medical care in Krakow is good and it is becoming a centre for 'medical tourists', who come from other countries for plastic surgery and dental treatment, which is more expensive in their home countries.

TIME DIFFERENCES

GMT	Krakow	Germany	USA (NY)	Netherlands	Spain
12 noon	1pm	1PM	7AM	1PM	1PM

Krakow is on Central European Time, in winter one hour ahead of GMT, six hours ahead of New York and nine hours ahead of Los Angeles. In summer, clocks go forward one hour.

NATIONAL HOLIDAYS

1 Jan New Year's Day	**15 Aug** Feast of the Assumption
1 May Labour Day	**1 Nov** All Saints' Day
3 May Constitution Day	**11 Nov** Independence Day
Ascension Day 40 days after Easter	**25 Dec** Christmas Day
Feast of Corpus Christi Thursday after Trinity Sunday	**26 Dec** Boxing Day

Many restaurants and a few of the shops that cater mainly for tourists will not close on public holidays, although banks and businesses will. However, at Christmas and Easter you will find most local people celebrating at home.

WHAT'S ON WHEN

January Carnival season.

February/March Lent: church ceremonies. Processions of hooded Brothers of the Good Death at the Franciscan church every Fri in Lent.

March/April Misteria Paschalia early music festival. Holy Week and Good Friday services. Bach Days music festival.

April All Fools' Day (1 Apr). Easter: Holy Saturday, church blessing of bread and food for families; Easter Sunday, family and church celebrations; Easter Monday, everyone splashes each other with water. Also Emaus festival, fair along ul. Kościuszki to the Rudawa

River; Easter Tuesday, Rękawka festival at Krak's Mound. Easter Beethoven music festival.

May Polish Flag Day (2 May). Constitution Day (3 May). Cracovia Marathon. St Stanislaw procession (Sun after 8 May) from Wawel to Skalka. Corpus Christi: procession with scattering of flower petals. Cracow Screen Festival. Juwenalia student festival. Night of Museums: special events. Lajkonik parade (Thu after Corpus Christi). Film Music Festival. Photography month: exhibitions citywide.

June Krakow Festival. Children's Day (1 Jun). Open Gardens Festival. Pageant to enthrone the cockerel king of the Brotherhood of Riflemen. Wianki Festival (24 Jun): floating wreaths with candles on the Vistula, all-night music and fireworks. Grand Dragon Parade.

July Festivals of Jewish culture, military bands, street theatre, jazz, Carpathian music.

August Folk festival. *Pierogi* food festival.

September Sacrum Profanum festival of contemporary music. Dachshund Parade.

October Month of Encounters with Jewish Culture. Organ Music Days. Krakow Book Fair

November All Saint's Day (1 Nov) and All Soul's Day (2 Nov): everyone visits cemeteries to put flowers and candles on the graves. Independence Day (11 Nov). Krakow's Christmas market opens on Rynek Główny (end Nov–Christmas Eve). Zaduszki jazz festival.

December Feast of Mikolaj (6 Dec), St Nicholas brings children gifts. Christmas cribs on show (morning of first Thu in Dec) in Rynek Główny; the best are exhibited until February at Krzysztofory Palace. Christmas Eve/Christmas Day are family days. Sylwester: New Year's Eve celebrations in the Old Town.

Getting there

BY AIR

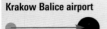

Krakow Balice airport

15km (9 miles) to cental Krakow

🚊 30 minutes

🚌 60 minutes

🚕 25 minutes

International flights arrive direct to Krakow's John Paul II International Airport at Balice from many cities in Europe and from North America. It is also well served by low-cost airlines. The airport is expanding and the timetable varies, so it is best to check on the airport website (www. lotnisko-balice.pl). Don't be tempted by low-cost airline claims to fly to Katowice, an industrial and business centre about an hour's drive from Krakow – the transfer is not easy.

You'll see desks for all the main car rental companies in the arrivals hall. If you are visiting Krakow only you are probably better without one.

The best ways to get into the city from the airport are by taxi or train. You can pick up a metered taxi from just outside the international arrivals terminal. The driver will give you a receipt *(paragon)* for the fare if you ask for it. It should take between 20 and 30 minutes to drive to the Old Town, and will cost you 50–60PLN. Alternatively, you can book a taxi with the airport's official company (tel: 9191). If your hotel or hostel offers to send a car to meet you, check the price. It can be a little cheaper than taking a taxi.

Or you can catch a shuttle bus, also from outside the international arrivals hall, for the train from the airport to the main station (Dworzec Główny). Trains leave once every 30 minutes and you can be in the city in under half an hour. Tickets (6PLN) are available on the train or before boarding.

As for local buses, the 292 (departures about every 40 minutes) takes about an hour to get into the city, but one of its many stops may be more convenient for where you are staying. Similarly, the 208 will take you to Nowy Kleparz for 2.60PLN one-way, with a 0.50PLN surcharge if you buy your ticket from the driver rather than from the machine at the bus stop.

BY RAIL

Krakow's Dworzec Główny railway station, just outside the Old Town, is well connected with the rest of Poland and other cities in Europe. Check out www.pkp.com.pl for routes, timetables and ticket information. For express and international trains see www.intercity.com.pl.

BY CAR

The main international motorways through Krakow are the A4 (from Germany through Wrocław, Katowice, Kraków, Tarnów and Rzeszów into the Ukraine) and the A7 from Gdańsk through Warsaw and Kraków to Slovakia. From Krakow it's 295km (183 miles) to Warsaw, 100km (62 miles) to Zakopane and 114km (71 miles) to Częstochowa.

BY BUS

The Regionalny Dworzec Austobusowy bus station is close to the train station (www.rda.krakow.pl). You can also get information from Eurolines, which runs international bus services to Krakow from several cities in Europe. For details of routes, ticket prices and 15- and 30-day European bus travel passes see its website – www.eurolines.com.

Getting around

BY FOOT

Most of what you'll want to see and do in Krakow can be easily reached by walking. The city is fairly flat and most of the sights are grouped close together in the Old Town or Kazimierz.

BUSES AND TRAMS

Krakow's efficient bus and tram service, which includes a night bus network, runs out from the Old Town to the inner city and the farthest suburbs (tel: MPK general 9285, information 9150; www.mpk.krakow. pl). Buy tickets from machines at stops, kiosks near stops or machines on some buses. Machines usually have information in English as well as Polish. Buying a ticket on board means you have to pay an extra 0.50PLN on the basic price of 2.50PLN. Validate your ticket by punching it in one of the orange machines on board and keep it for inspection.

MINIBUSES

You'll see minibuses around the Planty (➤ 127) running from the Old Town to Podgórze or Kazimierz and out to Wieliczka. These are privately run but well regulated. The destination is shown on the front and you pay the driver. Fares are roughly double those on official city buses. Many routes begin at the main railway station, or try the main post office.

TAXIS

Taxi fares are moderate and you'll find taxi ranks just within the Planty at Plac Szczepański, ul. Sienna, ul. Sławkowska and at the junction of ul. Stradomska and ul. Bernardyńska. To call for a taxi, tel: 012 9661 (Barbakan Taxi), 012 9664 (Euro Taxi), 012 9621 (City Taxi) or 012 9191 (Radio Taxi). Use only metered taxis, which are clearly marked.

CITY TOURS AND BEYOND

You can rent a minibus or taxi for all or part of a day. Prices are negotiable but usually fair, and your hotel and hostel will probably be able to recommend a reputable company. There are also regular all-day or half-day tours to popular sights which anyone can join and which might be an option if you are a single traveller.

CAR RENTAL

The Old Town is mostly pedestrianized. The roads in the area just outside the Planty are often one-way, parking is limited, public transport is good, taxis are moderate and most of the sights are within walking distance of each other, so if you are staying in Krakow it's best not to drive. If you're travelling further afield in Poland, you'll find a list of car rental companies on the city website – www.krakow.pl.

DRIVING

- Drive on the right.
- Your vehicle must carry a warning triangle, a fire extinguisher and a first-aid kit.
- You must always drive with the headlights on, night and day.
- Seatbelts must be worn in the front and rear of the vehicle.

- Speed limits are 50kph (31mph) in built-up areas, 90kph (56mph) outside those areas, 100kph (62mph) on A-class roads, 130kph (80mph) on motorways.
- Pedestrians take precedence at traffic lights.
- Beware heavy fines for parking without paying and displaying in controlled zones. Tow trucks are very active in Krakow.
- If you have an accident you must stay on the scene, give first aid to anyone injured, and call an ambulance or doctor and the police.

BOAT TOURS

In summer, between May and October, river cruisers moor at the bend of the Vistula between the Dębnicki and Grunwaldzki bridges. Trips can be anything from half an hour to half a day, which will take you as far as Bielany and Tyniec. Prices are moderate.

VISITORS WITH DISABILITIES

Many of the streets in the Old Town, originally cobbled and uneven, are being renovated to match the smoother, level surfaces of the Rynek Główny, but outside this small area, pavements and roads are often in a bad state of repair and kerbs are high. However, except for Wawel Hill, the Old Town and Kazimierz are fairly flat, though you'll find restaurants, bars and clubs are often in cellars. Galeria Stanczyk information centre for visitors with disabilities, tel: 012 636 8584; open Tue, Thu 11–5.

CYCLING

Cycling is a good way to see the city or get out into the countryside, and prices are reasonable. Eccentric Bike Tours & Rentals (tel: 012 430 2034; www.eccentric.pl) has all sorts or bicycles, or try Cruising Krakow (tel: 012 398 7057; 514 556 017; www.cruisingkrakow.com).

HORSE-DRAWN AND ELECTRIC CARTS

Take a horse and carriage around the Old Town. Prices vary according to the length of the ride, but it is expensive. A more reasonable, if less romantic, option is a Melex tour in one of the electric golf cart-style vehicles, which also wait for passengers in the Rynek Główny. They offer a variety of tours in the Old Town or out to Kazimierz and beyond, and usually feature a recorded commentary in the language of your choice.

Being there

TOURIST OFFICES
City Tourist Information Network
Town Hall Tower, 1 Rynek Główny
☎ 012 433 7310; www.krakow.pl
◉ Mon–Sun 9–7

International Airport Krakow-Balice
☎ 012 285 5341 ◉ Mon–Sun 10–6

25 ul. Szpitalna
☎ 012 432 0110 ◉ Mon–Sun 9–7

2 ul. św. Jana 2
☎ 012 421 7787 ◉ Mon–Sat 10–6

7 ul. Józefa, Kazimierz
☎ 012 422 0471 ◉ Mon–Sun 10–6

16 os. Słoneczne, Nowa Huta
☎ 012 643 0303 ◉ Tue–Sat 10–2

Wyspiański 2000 Pavilion,
2 Plac Wszystkich Świętych
☎ 012 616 1886 ◉ Mon–Sun 9–7

MONEY
The złoty is the official currency in Poland, usually abbreviated to zł or PLN. You'll find a good choice of bureaux de change, banks and cash machines in Krakow's Old Town and in Kazimierz. Everywhere in Krakow is well served with ATMs.

POSTAL AND INTERNET SERVICES
The city's main post office is at 20 ul. Westerplatte and is open Mon–Fri 7:30am–8:30pm, Sat 8–2. The post office near the railway station at 4 ul. Lubicz has some round-the-clock services, otherwise it's open Mon–Fri 7am–8pm. You can also buy stamps at kiosks. Post boxes

TIPS/GRATUITIES

Yes ✓ No ✗		
Restaurants (if service not included)	✓	10–15%
Cafés/bars (if service not included)	✓	10–15%
Taxis (for helpful service)	✓	10–15%
Porters	✓	5PLN
Chambermaids	✓	10PLN a day

are red with the symbol of a yellow horn in a blue disc and the words Poczta Polska.

Koffeina at 23 Rynek Główny is the most central cybercafé (www.cafe.studencki.pl), but there are many others in the Old Town, as well as bars and cafés offering free WiFi. The whole of the Rynek Główny and the centre of Kazimierz have free WiFi and all hostels and most hotels provide internet access. In older hotels, coverage can be patchy, so check when you book.

TELEPHONES

You can buy a local sim card for your mobile telephone at newsagents or kiosks, where you can also buy phone cards. When telephoning within the city you need to use the full Krakow code: 012. Also use the zero before the city code when telephoning other cities in Poland.

International dialling codes
UK: 00 44
Germany: 00 49
USA: 00 1
Netherlands: 00 31
Spain: 00 34

To call Krakow from abroad
From the UK dial: 00 48 12
From the US dial: 011 48 12

Emergency telephone numbers
Any emergency (including ambulance): 999
SOS by mobile/cellphone: 112

Police: 997
Fire: 998

EMBASSIES AND CONSULATES

UK ☎ 012 421 7030; www.britishembassy.gov.uk
Germany ☎ 012 424 30 00; www.krakau.diplo.de
USA ☎ 012 424 5183; www.krakow.usconsulate.gov
Netherlands ☎ 022 559 1200; www.nlembassy.pl
Spain ☎ 022 622 4250

ELECTRICITY

Like the rest of Europe, Poland uses a 220-volt system and round-pin plugs. Bring an adaptor. US visitors need to make sure their equipment is dual-voltage.

HEALTH AND SAFETY

Drugs For minor illnesses try a pharmacy *(apteka)* first. Many pharmacists speak good English.

Safe water Bottled water is widely available, but Krakow's tap water is safe to drink.

Personal safety

Krakow is a safe city with a strong, visible police presence in tourist areas, but as with any city, take care of your bags, money and other valuables, particularly in cafés and bars.

Equally, the police expect visitors to abide by the rules. These include no jaywalking, no littering, no public drunkenness or drinking alcohol on the street. Laws are enforced with on-the-spot fines and drunks are taken to a drying-out clinic overnight and charged for their stay.

OPENING HOURS

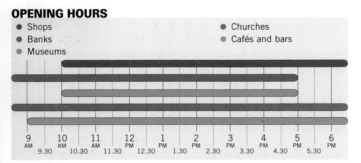

Shops catering for tourists keep longer hours, but most are open Mon–Fri 10–6 or 7, with later opening and earlier closing on Sat (as early as 2 or 3pm). Many but not all shops are open on Sun. There are many small convenience stores in the Old Town and nearby that are open 24 hours daily. Most museums are closed on Mon, otherwise opening hours of museums and tourist attractions vary widely, and many have longer hours in the summer than in the winter. Last entry is half an hour before closing. Banks are open Mon–Fri 8–5, Sat 8–1. Bars, cafés, clubs and restaurants serving a young, party-loving clientele will often open at 9am and stay open until the early hours of the next morning or 'until the last guest leaves' as is traditional in Krakow. Other establishments keep more moderate hours.

LANGUAGE

Krakow is full of people who speak English, but if you attempt to say a few words in Polish you will swiftly make friends. All Polish words are pronounced phonetically and the accent falls on the penultimate syllable.

yes/no	*tak/nie*	excuse me	*przepraszam*
please	*proszę*	help!	*pomocy!*
thank you	*dziękuję*	today	*dzisiaj*
good morning/		tomorrow	*jutro*
good afternoon	*dzień dobry*	yesterday	*wczoraj*
good evening	*dobry wieczór*	how much?	*ile to kosztuje?*
good night	*dobranoc*	open	*otwarty/czynny*
goodbye	*do widzenia*	closed	*zamknięty/nieczynny*
hotel	*hotel*	one/two	*jedna osoba/*
room	*pokój*	people	*dwie osoby*
… single	*… pojedynczy*	reservation	*rezerwacja*
… double	*… dwuosobowy*	rate	*cena*
one/two	*jeden doba (noc)/*	key	*klucz*
nights	*dwie dobe (nocy)*	breakfast	*śniadanie*
bank	*bank*	credit card	*karta kredytowa*
exchange office	*kantor*	foreign exchange	*wymiana walut*
post office	*poczta*	pound sterling	*funt szterling*
cashier	*kasjer/kasjerka*	American dollar	*dolar amerykański*
restaurant	*restauracja*	starter	*przystawka*
café	*kawiarnia*	main course	*główny danie*
menu	*karta/potraw*	dessert	*deser*
drink	*napój*	vegetarian	*wegetariański*
water	*woda*	the bill	*rachunek*
aeroplane	*samolot*	bus	*autobus*
airport	*lotnisko*	bus station	*dworzec autobusowy*
train	*pociąg*	ticket	*bilet*
train station	*dworzec*	… single	*… w jedną stronę/*
platform	*peron*	… return	*… powrotny*

Best places to see

1 Collegium Maius

www.uj.edu.pl/muzeum

There are many places of education in this university city, but this is the one that started it all in medieval times. Now it's a museum holding the college's treasures.

Legend has it that Queen Jadwiga sold her crown jewels to fund the revival of Krakow's university and the construction of this, its main building. King Kazimierz the Great had founded the first Krakow Academy in 1364, but it had lost prestige and power by the time the queen and her consort, King Władysław Jagiellon, came to the throne in 1384. Today, you join a tour to visit the museum, but first take a look at the clock

in the courtyard which plays the university song *Gaudeamus Igitur* several times a day while circled by academic characters carved in wood.

Upstairs, the Library's ceiling is a traditional skyscape, below which hang portraits of eminent scholars. The professors' rooms are furnished with period pieces, while items in the collection span 1,000 years of history. You'll see a charming wooden carving of King Kazimierz from about 1380, the Jagiellonian Globe, which was the first to depict the continent of America, 17th-century

Persian carpets and the only surviving drawing by Veit Stoss, the creator of the great altar in St Mary's Church. In the room dedicated to the astronomer Nicholas Copernicus, who studied here from 1491 to 1495 are a collection of astrolabes, including one made in Cordoba in 1054. More recently, another famous student, the film director Andrzej Wajda, donated his Oscar to the university museum. Fun for children is the separate, interactive World of the Senses science exhibition.

✠ 8D ✉ 15 ul. Jagiellońska
☎ 012 422 0549, 012 663 1307
🕐 Main exhibition: 30-min tours
Mon–Fri 10–2:20 (last tour), Sat 10–1:20 (last tour); Apr–Oct Thu last tour 17:20. Main exhibition plus scientific and fine arts collections: hour-long tour Mon–Fri only 1pm. Interactive science exhibition: Mon–Sat 9–1:30. Musical clock: daily 9, 11, 1, 3, 5 ✋ Main exhibition: inexpensive, free Apr–Sep Tue 3–5:20. Longer tour with scientific and fine arts collections: moderate. Interactive exhibition: inexpensive, Sat free 🍴 U Pęcherza cellar café (€) ❓ Advance booking recommended: main Collegium Maius tours ☎ 012 663 1521; interactive exhibition ☎ 012 663 1319

2 Dom Śląski

www.mhk.pl

Giving a vivid insight into life in Krakow under Nazi rule, this museum includes rooms that were once used as detention and torture cells.

31

This anonymous corner block on ul. Pomorska, initially built in the 1930s to provide accommodation for students from Silesia (Slaśk in Polish), was converted to deadly purpose as the Gestapo headquarters during World War II. Here prisoners were questioned and tortured; thousands died. Across the courtyard from the main museum, the cells have been preserved, their walls still carrying the inscriptions made by some 600 of the prisoners, sometimes written moments before they were killed.

The museum's permanent exhibition, Krakow 1939–56, is small but extremely comprehensive, with a mass of photographs and ephemera, including postcards showing the Nazi flag flying from buildings familiar to any tourist, and Rynek Główny renamed Adolf Hitler Platz. The archbishop of Krakow wrote to the Pope: 'Our situation is very tragic indeed. Deprived of almost all human rights, subject to the cruelty of people who in the majority do not have human feelings, we live in terrible fear and under incessant threat of losing everything in the event of displacement or deportation or of being imprisoned in the so-called concentration camp, from where only a few return alive.' Despite this terror, resistance flourished. The story is easy to follow in the clear English captions.

✚ 6B ✉ 2 ul. Pomorska ☎ 012 633 1414 🕐 Nov–Apr Tue, Thu–Sat and 2nd Sun of month 9–4, Wed 10–5; May–Oct Tue–Sat and 2nd Sun of month 10–5:30 ✋ Inexpensive 🚋 Tram 4, 14, 13, 24 to Plac Inwalidów

3 Katedra Wawełska

www.wawel.diecezja.pl

The centre of Christianity in Poland, Wawel Cathedral saw the coronations of all its kings and the funerals of many of its rulers and heroes.

Krakow's bishops came to Wawel Hill in about 1000AD and began the first of several churches here. The triple-aisled Gothic cathedral you see today was begun in 1320 and consecrated in 1364, but many of the chapels, such as the Renaissance Zygmunt chapel with its striking gold dome, were added later. As the burial place of St Stanisław, Poland's patron saint, now marked with an opulent silver tomb, the cathedral soon drew pilgrims, and Poland's kings made it a focus of church and state. In the main entrance hang huge bones, once rumoured to be those of the Wawel dragon, but really the remains of prehistoric beasts.

While the royal tombs are in the main cathedral, Poland's kings and queens are buried below in the crypt, as are some of the country's great soldiers, such as Tadeusz Kościuszko, known to Americans as well as Poles, and General Władysław Sikorski, leader of the Polish Government in Exile during World War II. You'll also find the graves of poets such as Adam Mickiewicz, and the altar where Karol Wojtyła, later to be John Paul II, the first Polish pope – said his first Mass. High above the cathedral, in the Zygmunt Tower, hangs the huge 11-tonne, 2m-wide (6.5ft) Zygmunt bell. Polish people believe if you touch it with your left hand you will be lucky in love.

✝ 8E ✉ Wawel 3 ☎ 012 429 3327; www.wawel.diecezja.pl 🕐 Apr–Sep Mon–Sat 9–5, Sun 12:30–5; Oct–Mar Mon–Sat 9–4, Sun 12:30–4. Museum Mon–Sat 9–5, closed Sun and holy days. Last ticket 3:45; last admission 1 hour before closing. Also closed 1 Jan, Maundy Thu, Good Fri, Easter Sat and Sun, 1 Nov, Sun in Advent, 24–25 Dec ✋ Inexpensive 🍴 Cafés on Wawel Hill (€) ❓ For more information, rent an audioguide

4 Kościół Mariacki

www.mariacki.com

The twin towers of St Mary's Church are the symbol of the city as much as the *hejnał* – the bugle call sounded hourly from the tallest tower.

Begun at the end of the 13th century, this Gothic marvel in red brick was not finished until the beginning of the 15th century, with side chapels and altars added down the centuries, including Renaissance tombs by Italian artists and murals and stained-glass windows from the turn of the 20th century. Inside, the highlight is the magnificent carved lindenwood altar by Veit Stoss, the Master of Nuremburg. Created between 1477 and 1489, it is the largest of its kind in Europe and its 200 gilded and painted figures are so detailed that a 20th-century Krakow professor was able to use it to study medieval skin diseases. As the finest sculptor of his time, Stoss was paid the equivalent of the city's budget for a whole year for his work.

You'll hear the *hejnał* wherever you are in the market square, but you can also climb the tower for a close-up – and good views over the city. The present-day buglers are carrying on a tradition that began in 1241 when a watchman raising the alarm of a Tatar attack on the city was hit in the throat by an arrow. He died, but the city was saved. In his memory, the bugle call is cut off in the middle of the last note. The sound of the *hejnał* is also used as a time-signal on Polish radio.

✚ 9D ✉ 5 Plac Mariacki ☎ 012 422 5518

🕐 Mon–Sat 11:30–6 (High Altar opens at 11:50), Sun 2–6, no visitors during Mass. Tower visits 3 May–Sep Tue, Thu, Sat, 9–11:30, 1–5:30

✋ Inexpensive 🍴 None ❓ Ticket office opposite side door on other side of Plac Mariacki. Tower tickets at base of tower

5 Muzeum Książąt Czartoryskich

www.muzeum-czartoryskich.
krakow.pl

www.czartoryski.org

**Star of the art collection of the
princely Czartoryski family is
Da Vinci's *Lady with an Ermine*,
but the riches of this gallery
also include a fine Rembrandt.**

Such is the troubled history of this
exceptional collection that it is
remarkable how much of it came
back to Poland. Princess Izabella
Czartoryska began
acquiring choice
pieces in the late 18th
century to preserve
some of Poland's
heritage, buying Turkish
trophies from the siege
of Vienna in 1683 and
royal treasures looted from
Wawel Castle in earlier
times. Her son, Prince Adam
Jerzy, found the Da Vinci and
a Raphael portrait of a young
man while travelling in Italy. The
romantic Izabella could not resist
adding the ashes of El Cid, scraps
from the grave of Romeo and Juliet

and relics of Abelard and Héloïse, and Petrach and Laura. Later political unrest caused the family to move to Paris with the collection, which by now included Rembrandt's *Landscape with a Good Samaritan*, where it stayed until 1876 when the city of Krakow, again enjoying more settled times, offered its former arsenal as a museum to house the collection.

In World War II, many of the best pieces were taken to Dresden, but eventually returned. However, during the war, the Nazis running the city took many of the best pieces for Hitler's private collection and incarcerated the curator in a concentration camp where he died. Some 844 items are still missing, including the Raphael portrait. An empty frame hangs on the wall near the Da Vinci, waiting for its return.

✚ 9C ✉ 19 ul. św. Jana; entrance also at 8 ul. Pijarska ☎ 012 422 5566 🕓 Tue–Sat 10–6, Sun 10–4; closed 1 Jan, Easter, 1 and 11 Nov, 24, 25, 31 Dec 💶 Inexpensive, Sun free

6 Muzeum Narodowe w Krakowie

www.muzeum.krakow.pl

Krakow's National Museum has the largest collection of 20th-century Polish art in the city, a floor of domestic arts and crafts and a gallery of military hardware.

On the top floor of this gallery are all the main names of Krakow's artistic life in the past hundred years. The stars of the Young Poland movement, which took place at the turn of the 20th century – Józef Mehoffer, Stanisław Wyspiański and Jan Matejko – are well represented here, as is the Modernist Stanisław Witkiewicz, known as Witkacy. He was a philosopher, novelist and playwright as well as a visual artist. Independence in 1920 encouraged the arts to flourish and, like Witkacy, artists looked beyond Poland's borders for new ideas. After 1945, the drive towards independence began again, as shown here in pieces by artists such as Tadeusz Kantor.

On the middle floor, the display of decorative arts and crafts stretches back to the early Middle Ages, with lovely silverware, stained glass and embroidery gathered from local churches. You'll also see a selection of 20th-century Polish crafts, showing the different traditional styles of costume and embroidery.

The Weapons and Colours in Poland exhibition on the ground floor also includes exhibits dating back to the Middle Ages, with the focus on the arms, armour and uniforms of the Polish military from the 18th century up to World War II.

✚ 6D ✉ 1 al. 3 Maja ☎ 012 295 5500 🕐 Tue–Sat 10–6, Sun 10–4 ✋ Inexpensive, Thu permanent exhibitions free 🍴 Café (€) 🚌 103, 114, 124, 164, 173, 179, 444 to the Cracovia Hotel. Tram 15, 18 to the Cracovia Hotel ❓ A combined ticket gives entry to all three permanent exhibitions for a little more than the price of two

Pałac Królewski na Wawelu

www.wawel.krakow.pl

Wawel Castle, a palace on the hill that overlooks Krakow, was the home of Poland's rulers down through the centuries, and is now restored to give a glimpse of past grandeur.

Although Poland's royal family first came to live on Wawel Hill in the 10th century, the Renaissance palace, with its arcaded, frescoed courtyard, was built in the early 16th century for King Alexander and his successor, Zygmunt the Old. Inside, the walls are hung with Brussels tapestries specially made for Zygmunt II Augustus, and many splendid paintings from the schools of Titian, Raphael and Botticelli. Though it was once the equal of any great palace in Europe, changes in Poland's fortunes meant many of its treasures were looted. At one stage the Austrian army used it as a barracks and stable. During the Nazi occupation of World War II, the tapestries and the 13th-century gold coronation sword – Szczerbiec – were kept safe in Canada.

Many of the grandly decorated State Rooms still have their carved and painted ceilings. The 30 lively wooden heads on the ceiling of the Deputies' Hall are what remains of the original 194. One is gagged, allegedly for telling the king what to do. It's worth visiting the Oriental Art exhibit, which shows the Eastern influences on Polish culture; the Armoury, which has Turkish tents, guns and armour captured by King Jan III Sobieski in the Battle of Vienna in 1683 and a rare Hussar suit of armour with feathered wings, and the Treasury, some of whose hoard of gold and gems goes back to the 2nd century BC.

🕇 8F ✉ Wawel 5 ☎ 012 422 51 55, ext 219 🌐 State Rooms: Apr–Oct Mon 9:30–1, Tue–Fri 9:30–5, Sat–Sun 11–6; Nov–Mar Tue–Sat 9:30–4, Sun 10–4. Royal Private Apartments Apr–Oct Tue–Fri 9:30–5, Sat–Sun 11–6; Nov–Mar Tue–Sat 9:30–4. Crown Treasury and Armoury: Apr–Oct Tue–Fri 9:30–5, Sat–Sun 11–6; Nov–Mar Tue–Sat 9:30–4, Sun 10–4; closed 1 and 3 May; 15 Aug Sun hours apply. All exhibits closed 1 Jan, Easter Sat and Sun, 1 and 11 Nov, 24–25 Dec 🖐 All tickets are timed. State Rooms: moderate, free tickets Mon Apr–Oct, Sun Nov–Mar, includes entry to Oriental Art exhibit. Royal Private Apartments: moderate. Crown Treasury and Armoury: moderate, free tickets Sun Nov–Mar 🍴 Wawel Hill cafés (€), shops, ATM and post office ❓ Two ticket offices (at Bernardyńska Gate and Herbowa or Coat of Arms Gate); close 1 hour 15 mins before exhibitions. Last admission 1 hour before closing. The arcaded courtyard closes 30 mins before the gates to Wawel Hill, which are open from 6am to dusk. For conservation reasons a limited number of tickets is on sale each day. To ensure entry, reserve timed tickets in advance for a moderate fee ☎ 012 422 1697 or download a form from the website and email it to bot@wawel.org.pl

8 Smocza Jama

www.wawel.krakow.pl

Once there was a dragon, or Smok, who lived in a cave under Wawel Hill – and the rest of the story is the legend of Krakow's earliest beginnings.

You'll see images of a dragon everywhere in Krakow, recalling the story of the days when people first settled the land beside the Vistula River. It's said their king, Krak, built a castle on Wawel Hill, but was soon troubled by a dragon which terrified the people by seizing livestock and young women to take back to its den and eat. As kings so often did, Krak offered the hand of his daughter Wanda, and with her his kingdom, to anyone who could kill the evil beast. Knights came and went, each one dying without defeating the creature.

Eventually, a young shoemaker offered to try his luck. He put together a trap made from fat, sulphur and sheepskin, disguised as a fleecy ram, which he left outside the dragon's lair. At dawn the dragon awoke and swallowed the sheep bait for breakfast. As the sulphur burned in its stomach, the dragon drank deep in the river

to try to put out the fire, but he drank so much that he exploded. And the shoemaker, the princess and all the people lived happily ever after.

Today the dragon lives again, as a statue by Bronisław Chromy that breathes real flames. You can pay to climb down inside the dragon's den from the top of Wawel Hill, or just walk along the riverbank to see it.

✚ 18H ✉ Wawel Hill ☎ 012 422 51 55, 012 422 61 21 🕐 Cave: Apr–Oct daily 10–5; Jul–Aug daily 10–6; closed Nov–Mar 👋 Inexpensive, under-7s free 🍴 Cafés on Wawel Hill (€)

Stara Synagoga

www.mhk.pl

This Renaissance building in the middle of Kazimierz is Poland's oldest surviving synagogue, now a museum of the rich Jewish heritage of the area.

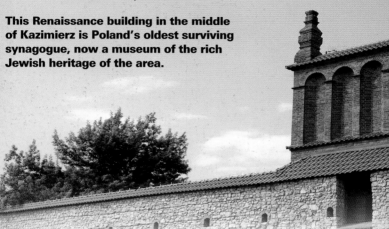

The first synagogue on this site was built in 1407 and formed part of the Kazimierz city walls. The Florentine architect Matteo Gucci kept some of its brick-ribbed vaulting when he redesigned the structure in 1570. Other sections, used for women's prayer and administration of the community, were added later, in the 16th and 17th centuries. During World War II, Krakow's Nazi governor Hans Frank took the synagogue's chandeliers and turned the building into a warehouse. The vaulting collapsed and it remained in ruins until restoration into a museum began in the 1950s.

Today you can still see the synagogue's original late-Renaissance stone Ark, as well as a baroque alms box dating from 1638 inside the main entrance. The bimah in the main prayer hall, with a wrought-iron canopy over a 12-sided stone base, is a replica of the 16th-century original. Among the displays are a scroll with the text of the Torah, items used on

Jewish holidays, including plates for the Passover bread and kiddush cups used on the Sabbath, a menorah, photographs of the traditional religious life and a collection of drawings and paintings of the streets of old Kazimierz. Outside, a plaque in the pavement commemorates the spot where Tadeusz Kościuszko called Kazimierz to fight for Polish independence in 1794.

✚ 21H ✉ 24 ul. Szeroka ☎ 012 422 0962, 012 431 05 45 🕐 Nov–Mar Mon 10–2, Wed–Thu, Sat–Sun 9–4, Fri 10–5; Apr–Oct Mon 10–2, Tue–Sun 9–5 ✋ Inexpensive, Mon free 🚋 Tram 3, 6, 9, 13, to Miodowa ❓ English audioguide inexpensive

10 Sukiennice

In the middle of the main market square, Krakow's Cloth Hall is still trading as it has done since the 13th century, though today it specializes in souvenirs not silks.

The medieval equivalent of a shopping mall, the Sukiennice is more than 100m (330yds) long and has always been at the heart of the commercial life of a city which grew on trade. The first Cloth Hall, built in the reign of Kazimierz the Great in the 14th century, was replaced after a fire in the 16th century by the current Renaissance building, decorated with gargoyles. Over the years, other market stalls and little shops grew up around it. The clear square you see today is the result of a 19th-century clean-up, when the female flower-sellers were the only stallholders outside the Sukiennice allowed to remain in the square.

Today you'll find stallholders in the Sukiennice selling jewellery in amber and silver, leather bags, sheepskins, linen, embroidered Polish folk costumes, stained-glass angels, decorated wooden boxes and carved wooden figures, as well as fluffy toy dragons and small knick-knacks for children. Look for the knife hanging on an entrance wall, said to be the one that the jealous builder of St Mary's Watchtower used to kill his brother, who built the Belltower.

The gallery of 19th-century Polish art featuring about 500 paintings and sculptures usually displayed on the upper floor has been moved to the Royal Castle at Niepołomice, while the restoration work continues.

➕ 8D ✉ 1–3 Rynek Główny ☎ None 🎁 Souvenir stalls daily 10–8 🖐 Free 🍴 Cafés in the arcades (€) ❓ The Sukiennice gallery will be at the Royal Castle at Niepołomice until at least 2010; daily 10–5 ☎ 012 261 9851; www.muzeum.niepolomice.pl 🖐 Inexpensive 🚐 Minibuses leave from opposite the main post office in ul. Starowiślna

Best things to do

Top activities

Climb high: take in the view from the top of the Town Hall Tower (► 101) or the bugler's eyrie at the top of St Mary's watchtower (► 42–43).

Go low: lower even than the cellar bars of the Old Town, the Wieliczka salt mines (► 146) are anything but grim. Deep underground you'll find vast caverns with soaring ceilings and remarkable carvings as you follow in the footsteps of famous visitors over the centuries – from the poet Goethe to the then President George Bush (senior) to Deep Purple's Ritchie Blackmore.

Head out: cycle along the the path beside the Vistula towards the abbey at Tyniec (► 148).

Sample the local firewater: try a *Tatanka* – bisongrass vodka with a dash of apple juice – or a straight shot of one of the many other flavoured vodkas. Your bartender or fellow drinkers will tell you their favourites. But go easy – it's strong stuff.

Give another culture a whirl: every evening in the former Jewish district of Kazimierz, you'll hear the strains of wild *klezmer* music on the air. Visit one of the many restaurants where *klezmer* bands play and experience the joyous emotion of the music.

Be a hero: confront the fiery flames breathed by the fierce dragon who lives under Wawel Hill (► 50–51).

Wave: to the *hejnał* bugler sounding the hour with a broken trumpet call from the highest tower of St Mary's Church (► 42–43). If he catches sight of you he'll probably wave back.

Count the animals: within the Old Town many houses are known by the sign over the door. You should be able to find Dom Pod Baranami (► 90–91), the House under the sign of the Rams – and there are fighting lizards, a rhino, an elephant and a white eagle if you look hard enough.

Take to the water: in summer there's a choice of boat rides along the river. Take your pick from the craft moored on the bend under Wawel Hill.

Feel the Earth move: In the church of SS Peter and Paul (► 83) there is an example of Foucault's pendulum – a device that shows the rotational movement of the Earth.

Best churches

Katedra Wawelska (► 40–41), chosen by kings

Kościół św. Andrzeja (► 79), one of the oldest buildings in town, for resisting the Tatar invaders

Kościół św. Anny (► 80), for over-the-top baroque

Kościół Franciszkanów (► 81), for its flower-painted walls and Modernist stained glass

Kościół św. Krzyża (► 83), for its unusual central pillar

Kościół Mariacki (► 42–43), for the highest of high Gothic

Kościół Paulinów na Skałce (► 130), for the tombs of the great and good in the crypt

Kościół Pijarów (► 83), for its trompe-l'oeil interior

Kościół św. Piotra i Pawła (► 83), for the Apostles guarding the entrance

Kościół św. Wojciecha (► 84), the tiniest church

Best museums

Collegium Maius: The museum in the first college of Krakow's first university brings together such disparate treasures as Andrzej Wajda's Oscar and Copernicus's astrolabes (➤ 36–37).

Dom Śląski: This chilling but essential history of wartime Krakow resistance includes some of the actual prison cells used by the Gestapo (➤ 38–39).

Muzeum Dom Mehoffera: The charming house of Józef Mehoffer, one of Krakow's great Modernist artists and also a great collector, has a very relaxing garden attached (➤ 132).

Muzeum Farmacje: You don't have to be a hypochondriac to enjoy this collection devoted to the apothecary's art down through the ages (► 86–87).

Muzeum Historii Fotografii: Even revolutionaries like to have their pictures taken, and this exhibition of the history of photography proves it (► 132–133).

Muzeum Inżynierii Miejskiej: Rows and rows of vintage cars and buses all housed in the city's former bus garage and tramshed will delight any petrolhead (► 115).

Muzeum Książąt Czartoryskich: This collection, begun by a princess, was moved around Europe to escape wars, but now almost all of its pieces are in their rightful place (► 44–45).

Pałac Biskupa Ezrama Ciołka: An old bishop's palace beautifully restored in Krakow's oldest street has a selection of lovely wooden carvings from the churches of the region (► 88–89).

Pałac Królewski na Wawelu: The kings' palace on Wawel Hill has ceilings carved with lifelike face, serried ranks of captured Turkish tents, and the 13th-century gold coronation sword, Szczerbiec (► 48–49).

Pałac Krzysztofory: The Historical Museum of Krakow comes into its own each December with its display of marvellously glittering Christmas cribs, many in the shape of Krakow's most celebrated buildings (► 90).

Stara Synagoga: The oldest synagogue in Poland gives a snapshot of the religious life in Kazimierz before World War II (► 52–53).

a walk around the Rynek Główny

This is a walk you can almost do with your eyes if your feet are saying 'no more'. Pick a café table with a good vantage point of the square and you'll be able to spot the main sights. But do try to get a close-up view by strolling along the sides of the square at some point in your stay – it's partly the wealth of historical detail on its venerable buildings that makes Krakow so special.

With your back to the giant bronze face by Igor Mitoraj, walk behind the Town Hall Tower (▶ 101) and left towards ul. Grodzka. On this side of the square are some of the grandest houses.

Many of the buildings of the Old Town, known as *kamienice*, were the palaces or town houses of noblemen. Some of the best are in the Rynek Główny

At the corner of ul. Grodzka look right down the Royal Route towards Wawel Hill. To your left is the tiny church of St Adalbert (▶ 84). Cross ul. Grodzka and walk left up the side of the square.

As you pass notice the intellectuals' hang-out Pod Jaszczurami (▶ 69), with its emblem of fighting lizards and glance into the 'Alkohole' shop at No 7 – its vaulted ceiling is almost as lovely as that in the Restauracja Szara next door. If you have children with you, see how many house emblems you can find – high up on the buildings as well as above the doorways.

Before you reach St Mary's Church (➤ 42–43) look right into the little square where you'll see a fountain with a statue of a medieval student, a modern copy of one of the figures from Veit Stoss's High Altar. To your left is the statue of Adam Mickiewicz (➤ 92–93). You're now walking towards ul. Floriańska, the other half of the Royal Route, which offers a splendid vista ending in Florian's Gate (➤ 74–75) and the Barbican (➤ 74).

At ul. Floriańska turn left and continue along the side of the square.

Notice the newly and splendidly restored Bonerowski Palace. There's a plaque on the wall detailing its history, which is fairly typical of such *kamienice*.

Turning left at the Krzysztofory Palace (➤ 90), make your way down the last side of the square.

Opposite the end of ul. Szewska, you'll find a paving stone set into the square showing where Kościuszko swore to serve his nation at the start of the 1794 Krakow uprising.

Finish by making your way towards Dom Pod Baranami, the House under the Sign of the Rams (➤ 90), on the corner of ul. św. Anny.

Distance 800m (0.5 miles)
Time 45 mins–2 hours
Start/end point Wieża Ratuszowa ✚ 8D
Lunch Kawiarnia Ratuszowa (€) ✉ 1 Rynek Główny ☎ 012 421 1326
🕔 Daily 9am–3am

Best souvenir buys

Amber: Baltic amber, the solidified resin of prehistoric pine trees, has been traded here since the earliest times, and was even found in Tutankhamun's tomb.

Carved wooden figures: The countryside around Krakow has a strong tradition of naïf artists, and their figures of local characters and idiosyncratic birds are very collectable.

Contemporary silver jewellery: Krakow is one of the country's premier artistic centres, which results in a great selection of imaginatively designed pieces for sale.

Crystal and glass: You'll need to be careful packing this, but handmade glass is perhaps the most typical example of Polish craft you can bring home.

Leather goods: The bags you'll see on sale in Krakow are certainly not designer, but will be well-made of good leather in classic shapes.

Linen and embroidery: Perhaps you don't want a traditional embroidered folk costume, but the table linen is a good buy.

Posters: One of these affordable masterpieces hanging in your home will be a colourful reminder of your visit.

Sheepskins: As a bedside rug or to wrap your baby in.

Stained-glass decorations: Too pretty to save for Christmas, stained-glass angels can catch the light in a window year-round.

Wooden boxes: Usually carved and painted, these make a useful and decorative gift.

Great cafés, bars and clubs

Alchemia

With candles providing the light, and seats from cinemas or old ladies' attics, Alchemia sums up bohemian Kazimierz. Reservations recommended for concerts, films, gigs in the Music Hall.

✉ 5 ul. Estery ☎ 012 428 4780; www.alchemia.com.pl ⚫ Daily 9am–4 or 5am

Café Gołębia (€)

A torchbearer of the individualism that defines a proper Krakow café. Post a poem in the blue *poczta poetycka* postbox outside and see if it's chosen to be put in the window.

✉ 3 ul. Gołębia ☎ 012 430 2419 ⚫ Daily 9am–11pm

Café Larousse (€)

Did you ever wish you were a character in a book? In this tiny café serving homemade cake you will be. The walls are pasted with pages plucked from 19th-century illustrated volumes.

✉ 22 ul. św. Tomasza ⚫ Daily 9–9

Café Philo

Make new friends in this crowded, chatty, Old Town bar, where debate is often lively.

✉ 30 ul. św. Tomasza ⏰ 10am–last guest leaves

Europejska (€€)

An incongruous English phonebox and French horn form part of the decor of this otherwise smart café, which harks back to the days when everyone waltzed in the evening.

✉ 35 Rynek Główny ☎ 012 429 3493 ⏰ Daily 8am–midnight

Imbir Music Club

An amazingly varied live music policy from highland folk singers to jazz to pop. DJs and dancing, too.

✉ 35 św. Tomasza ☎ 012 802 9241 ⏰ Daily 5pm–'infinity'

Pod Jaszczurami

This student-style bar 'Under the Lizards' is alive with debates, lectures, films, music and happenings.

✉ 8 Rynek Główny ☎ 012 292 2202; www.podjaszczurami.pl ⏰ Mon–Wed 10am–1am; disco nights Thu–Sat 10am–4am, Sun 11am–1am

Pub Propaganda

This music club is a cult and if you like your walls hung with Communist gewgaws and portraits of Lenin you'll want to join.

✉ 20 ul. Miodowa ☎ 012 292 0402; www.propaganda.biz.pl ⏰ Daily 11am–last guest

Singer

One of Kazimierz's defining cafés – they thought of the lace and old sewing machine look first, and they're not about to give it up.

✉ 20 ul. Estery/1 ul. Izaaka ☎ 012 292 0622 ⏰ Daily 9am–last guest leaves

Exploring

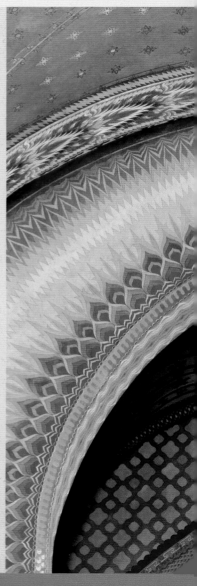

Krakow is a city with a strong, individual character. With an illustrious history as the the seat of archbishops and kings, it retained its personality even when, under partition, Poland ceased to exist for a couple of centuries.

The arts and architecture have always been important here. From the work of the Master Carver of Nuremburg, Veit Stoss, who made St Mary's altar, to the many Italian architects who created the city's baroque churches and palaces, to the contemporary violin virtuoso Nigel Kennedy, artists have chosen Krakow as their creative home.

Hand-in-hand goes academic life. From the time of the Krakow Academy, founded in 1364, to today's multitude of learning institutions, students energize the old place, and keep it buzzing. Even the Kazimierz, the former Jewish district, whose citizens were wiped out in wartime, is finding a new role, while celebrating its old one.

The Old Town and Wawel

At first glance, the Old Town appears to be a slice of living history – beautiful medieval, Renaissance and baroque buildings restored as designer hotels, traditional restaurants and cafés of great character.

Yet underground, wild music and creative happenings stir in late-night cellar bars frequented by students, while on Wawel Hill, the castle and cathedral remind us this was once a capital city.

BARBAKAN

Krakow's 15th-century Barbican, one of the best-preserved
medieval fortifications you are likely to see anywhere, stands
on what was the most important trade route into the city and
protected the Royal Route to Wawel Hill. Originally part of the city
walls, today it stands alone, looking like a child's fort. You'll get
good views of the Planty and the city from the upper galleries,
and in summer (Jun–Sep) medieval pageants and knightly
combats are held here regularly.

www.mhk.pl

🕂 9C ✉ ul. Basztowa ☎ 012 619 2320 ⏰ 15 Apr–Oct daily 10:30–6; closed
winter ✋ The inexpensive ticket also gives entry to the city walls and the
Celestat Museum of the Marksmen's Guild

BRAMA FLORIAŃSKA

From 1300 onwards, future kings of Poland entered the city on
their way to be crowned at Wawel Cathedral through Florian's
Gate. The little that remains of the city walls stretches out either

side of it. Here visitors can learn from a series of explanations in English how each guild of city tradesmen, such as haberdashers and carpenters, took control of one of the towers in the wall and defended the city from attack in times of need. These amateurs were trained by the Marksmen's Guild, still an important organization in the city today.

www.mhk.pl

✚ 9C ✉ ul. Floriańska ☎ 012 619 2320 🕐 Gate always open; city walls, 15 Apr–Oct daily 10:30–6; closed winter ✋ Gate free, city walls inexpensive. Ticket also gives entry to the city walls and the Celestat Museum of the Marksmen's Guild

CASTLE WALLS

It can be difficult to tell which of the walls and towers that surround Wawel Hill are defensive and which are part of the fabric of the cathedral and castle. Farthest away, when looking from the Old Town, are the cathedral's baroque Clock Tower,

Zygmunt Tower and Silver Bells Tower. From the east, you can see the Gothic Jordanka, the Danish Tower and Kurza Stopka or Hen's Foot Tower, with the baroque Zygmunt III Tower at the corner of the castle. The three tall brick towers nearer to the river are the Baszta Złodzieska or Thieves' Tower, Baszta Sandomierska or Sandomierz Tower, and the Senators' Tower or Lubranka. Star-shaped fortifications were added on the river side of the hill in the 18th century.

www.wawel.krakow.pl

✚ 8F ✉ Wawel Hill ☎ 012 422 51 55 ✋ Free

COLLEGIUM IURIDICUM

Half-way down ul. Grodzka, a 17th-century doorway invites exploration. Inside you'll find modern sculpture by Igor Mitoraj in the colonnaded courtyard of a university building rebuilt several times since its first incarnation as part of Queen Jadwiga's bequest to the Krakow Academy, most recently in 1719. You can visit the Jagiellonian University's Natural History Museum, across the courtyard, which has thousands of marine shells, fossils and butterflies, or in summer take in a concert in the courtyard itself.

🚹 8E ✉️ 56 ul. Grodzka ☎️ 012 422 7711 🕐 Courtyard: daily 7:45am–8pm; museum: Mon–Fri 10–6, Sat 10–3, Sun 11–3 ✋ Free

COLLEGIUM MAIUS

Best places to see, ➤ 36–37.

COLLEGIUM NOVUM

Echoing in style the much older Collegium Maius, this imposing, red-brick university building on the site of the 15th-century Jerusalem and Philosophers' halls of residence dates from the 1880s. Sometimes you'll see groups of students and academics gathered outside since all the university's ceremonies take place in its Aula Magna, or Great Hall. If you are not graduating, your best chance of seeing the interior is by attending a concert.

🚹 8D ✉️ 24 ul. Gołębia 🕐 Not open to tourists; view outside only from the Planty, unless attending a concert

DOROŻKI

Krakow's cherished horse-drawn cabs, lined up near the flower stalls day and night, winter and summer, are much celebrated in poetry and legend. If you decide to take a ride, pick whichever one in the rank takes your fancy; there's no need to take the first, but discuss the route with the driver. You'll see the horses

are well cared-for – not only are they decorated with gorgeous trappings and tassels, they are shod with special rubber shoes to protect their hooves on the cobbled streets.

✚ 8D ✉ Rynek Główny ☎ 012 431 2520; www.dorozki.krakow.pl is one company, office hours Mon–Fri 10–5 🕐 Daily early morning until the small hours ✋ Expensive–very expensive. The price depends on the length of the journey: the shortest is around the main square, about 70PLN, the longest is a round-trip to Wawel and Kazimierz, about 250PLN 🍴 Cafés nearby

JAMA MICHALIKA

In a city rich in café culture, this one stands out, although these days its allure is mainly historic. 'Michael's Den' was set up in 1895 and soon became a haunt of artists, bohemians and intellectuals, as well as the home of Zielony Balonik, the Green Balloon satirical cabaret. You'll see their art and cariacatures on the walls, and sit on the original art nouveau furniture.

www.jamamichalika.pl

✛ 9C ✉ 45 ul. Floriańska ☎ 012 422 1561 🕔 Sun–Thu 9am–10pm Fri–Sat 9am–11pm 🍴 Café (€)

KAMIENICA HIPOLITÓW

Tucked away just off the Rynek Główny, this museum illustrates how life was lived in the grand houses of the Old Town between the 17th and 19th centuries. Its rooms are furnished for every member of the family, and the overall effect is rich and textured. Among the masses of ornaments and pictures, the little human touches – baby bootees or a child's homework – are engaging.

www.mhk.pl

✛ 9D ✉ 3 Plac Mariacki ☎ 012 422 4219 🕔 May–Oct Wed–Sun 10–5:30; 2 Nov–30 Apr Wed, Fri, Sat, Sun 9–4, Thu 12–7. Closed Mon and Tue and 2nd Sun of month ✋ Inexpensive, free Wed all year 🍴 Magia café at entrance (€)

KATEDRA WAWELSKA

Best places to see, ➤ 40–41.

KOŚCIÓŁ ŚW. ANDRZEJA

St Andrew's stands out in a city almost completely built in Gothic and later styles. As the only church to survive when a Tatar invasion laid waste to the city in 1241, its 11th-century Romanesque lines look very plain compared with Krakow's more usual ecclesiastical extravagance, even though its two white towers later gained baroque cupolas. There's more baroque to see inside, with stuccowork by Baldassare Fontana.

✛ 9E ✉ 56 ul. Grodzka 🕔 Daily 7:30–5 ✋ Free 🍴 Café nearby

KOŚCIÓŁ ŚW. ANNY

Built at the end of the 17th century, the university church of St Anne's is a soaring example of high baroque, perhaps the best in a city which provides a lot of competition. Baldassare Fontana created the main altar, dedicated to św. Jan Kęnty, a professor and saint who was buried here in 1473, while the pulpit, supported by gold angels, and the gilded and painted cupola are other highlights among the dazzling riot of decoration.

www.kolegiata-anna.diecezja.krakow.pl

➕ 8D ✉ 11 ul. św. Anny ☎ 012 422 5318 🕐 Daily 7am–9pm ✋ Free 🍴 Cafés nearby

KOŚCIÓŁ ŚW. BARBARY

Situated next to St Mary's, St Barbara's church dates from the end of the 14th century and is said to have been built with the

bricks left over from the construction of its grand neighbour. Among the treasures inside are a crucifix on the high altar and a pietà, both dating from the 15th century. Restoration work has already enhanced the beautifully painted ceiling and is continuing.

✛ 9D ✉ 8 Mały Rynek ☎ None ◷ Daily according to the times of services; German Mass Sun 7pm ✋ Free 🍴 Many cafés nearby

KOŚCIÓŁ FRANCISZKANÓW

The Franciscan Church, rebuilt several times since it was founded in the 13th century, was almost destroyed in the great fire of 1850, giving the leading artists of the day a chance to raise it again. The cloisters still have murals in Gothic, Renaissance and baroque styles, but the main body of the church was painted with stylized Modernist flowers by Stanisław Wyspiański. He also designed the dramatic stained-glass window – God the Father – over the main entrance; at different times of the day it changes colour as the light strikes it. Look for Jósef Mehoffer's 1933 Stations of the Cross and the 16th-century Mater Dolorosa by Master Jerzy.

www.franciszkanska.pl

✛ 8D ✉ 5 Plac Wszystkich Świętych ☎ 012 422 5376 ◷ Daily 6am–7:45pm ✋ Free

CHRISTO TRANSFIGURATO

KOŚCIÓŁ ŚW. KRZYŻA

The Church of the Holy Cross is like a Gothic tree built in brick – the ribbed vaulting of the interior is supported by a single pillar in the centre. The church itself is well preserved, with 15th- to 17th-century wall paintings restored by Wyspiański, a 15th-century font and a baroque altar and choirstalls.

✚ 9C ✉ 23 ul. św. Krzyża ☎ 012 429 2056 ◷ Mon–Sat 7:30–6:30, Sun 7:30am–9:30pm

KOŚCIÓŁ MARIACKI

Best places to see, ➤ 42–43.

KOŚCIÓŁ PIJARÓW

The 18th-century Piarist Church has an unusual rococo facade added by Francesco Placidi about 30 years after the church was built by Kasper Bażanka, who was not only a Rome-trained architect but also became mayor of Krakow. The interior is a colourful exuberance of trompe l'oeil painting by Franz Eckstein, while the crypt, whose entrance is directly beneath the main doors, is often used for concerts and exhibitions.

✚ 9C ✉ 2 ul. Pijarska ◷ Daily 7–7

KOŚCIÓŁ ŚW. PIOTRA I PAWŁA

SS Peter and Paul, the first completely baroque church in Poland, was consecrated in 1635 and is distinctive because of the line of statues of the Apostles which mark its frontage on ul. Grodzka and which were erected to conceal the fact that the church stands at an angle to the street. Inside, the baroque style is continued in stuccowork by Falconi above the high altar showing scenes from the lives of the saints, highly decorated tombs and the organ loft. The Jesuit preacher Piotr Skarga, whose statue stands on a pillar in Plac św. Marii Magdaleny, opposite the church, is buried in the crypt. Look for the model of Foucault's Pendulum, which demonstrates the rotation of the Earth.

✚ 9E ✉ 54 ul. Grodzka ◷ Daily 7–7, later for concerts; demonstration of Foucault's Pendulum Thu 10, 11 and 12

KOŚCIÓŁ ŚW. WOJCIECHA

This little baroque church, sitting on Romanesque foundations, is one of the oldest buildings in Krakow. It is much used by locals who like to drop in for a quiet prayer away from the hubbub of the main market square. You can see everything inside from a seat in a rear pew, including the image of the church's patron saint, the missionary św. Wojciech, whose name is usually translated into English as St Adalbert. A small archaeology museum underneath the church shows finds from the church and square in summer when the weather is not too damp.

www.ma.krakow.pl

✚ 8D ✉ 3 Rynek Główny ☎ 012 422 7100; www.diecezja.pl 🕐 Daily 7–7. Museum: Jun–Sep daily 10–4, but often closed if wet ✋ Museum: inexpensive 🍴 Cafés in the square

KRZYŻ KATYŃSKI

The simple wooden cross standing outside the

14th-century Kościół św. Idziego (St Giles' Church) at the end of ul. Grodzka is a memorial to a tragedy in Poland's more recent history. It commemorates the murder in the Katyń forest in March 1940 of some 22,000 Polish officers, among them many academics, doctors and lawyers, by Russian troops acting on the orders of Stalin, who intended to wipe out the nation's leaders.

✚ 8E ✉ 1 ul. św. Idziego

MUZEUM ARCHEOLOGICZNE

While specializing in finds from Poland and its neighbours and concentrating on discoveries from the Malopolska region, the Archaeological Museum does not neglect world-class crowd-pleasers such as Egyptian mummies. Look for mammoth bones, 3rd-century BC golden treasure from the Ukraine, and Światowid, an early pagan idol resembling a stone totem pole, dredged up from a nearby stream. The garden bordering the Planty is a quiet place to relax on a summer's day.

www.ma.krakow.pl

➕ 8E ✉ 3 ul. Senacka; enter from 3 ul. Poselska ☎ 012 422 7100
🕓 Jul–Aug Mon, Wed, Fri 9–2, Tue, Thu 2–6, Sun 10–2; Sep–Jun Mon–Wed 9–2, Thu 2–6, Fri, Sun 10–2 ✋ Inexpensive, Sun permanent exhibition free; English audioguide inexpensive; garden inexpensive

MUZEUM DOM POD KRZYŻEM

The House under the Cross, a grand Renaissance building previously used as a hospital and a monastery, has most recently been a museum featuring an exhibition about the history of theatre in Krakow. It is currently being renovated.

www.mhk.pl

✚ 9D ✉ 21 ul. Szpitalna ☎ 012 422 6864 ⊘ Currently closed

MUZEUM FARMACJE

Krakow's Pharmacy Museum is a surprisingly charming and interesting place, with its world-class collection of examples of the apothecary's art in a beautiful Renaissance building. Highlights among its 22,000 exhibits are the alchemist's laboratory in the cellar, complete with dried bats and crocodiles.

Faust is said to have studied at the Jagiellonian University, though it's not known whether it was here that he made his pact with the Devil. From here, up to the herbs drying in the attic, past the jars of leeches and pickled snakes, it's a fascinating archive of pills, potions and instruments.

www.uj.edu.pl

➕ 9D ✉ 25 ul. Floriańska ☎ 012 421 9279 🕐 Tue 12–6:30, Wed–Sun 12–2:30 ✋ Inexpensive

MUZEUM KSIĄŻĄT CZARTORYSKICH

Best places to see, ➤ 44–45.

MUZEUM WYSPIAŃSKIEGO

The name of Stanisław Wyspiański crops up everywhere in Krakow. A painter, playwright, sculptor, designer and professor, he was born here in 1869, and by the time he died in 1907 he had made an indelible mark on every aspect of creativity in the city. His play *Wesele (The Wedding)*, is still much performed. His versatility is displayed in exhibits such as his model for a (never realized) 'Polish Acropolis' on Wawel Hill, paintings of the city and prominent characters of his day, designs for interiors, stained-glass windows and even a costume for the Lajkonik folk figure that is still in use. Several rooms are devoted to Feliks 'Manggha' Jasieński, the collector who introduced Wyspiański and other members of the Young Poland movement to Japanese art.

www.muzeum.krakow.pl

➕ 8D ✉ 11 ul. Szczepańska ☎ 012 292 8183, 012 422 7021 🕐 May–Oct Wed–Sat 10–6, Sun 10–4; Nov–Apr Tue–Thu, Sat–Sun 10–3:30, Fri 10–6 ✋ Inexpensive; permanent exhibition free Sun May–Oct, Thu Nov–Apr 🍴 Café Pod Kasztanowcem (€), closed Mon–Tue ❓ Photography and filming moderate fee

PAŁAC BISKUPA EZRAMA CIOŁKA

Entry to the courtyard is free if you just want to admire the medieval and Renaissance details of the architecture of this palace in Krakow's oldest and best preserved street, but it's worth venturing in to see the excellent collections of the Art of Old Poland and the Orthodox Art of the Polish-Lithuanian Republic. The first is composed of many coloured wooden figures of saints and madonnas carved between the 14th and the 16th centuries and discovered in churches in the region, while the second comprises a priceless collection of 15th- and 16th-century

Carpathian icons, together with later icons showing Renaissance and baroque influences. Look for the 16th-century statue of Christ riding a donkey, the early 15th-century Madonna of Krużlowa and the Padovano angels. Next door, in the **Archdiocesan Museum,** is a reconstruction of the rooms at No 21 where Karol Wojtyła lived before he became Pope, while opposite at No 18 is the new John Paul II Centre (www.janpawel2.pl).

www.muzeum.krakow.pl

✚ 8E ✉ 17 ul. Kanonicza ☎ 012 429 1558, 012 424 9370 🕓 May–Oct Tue–Sat 10–6, Sun 10–4; Nov–Apr Tue–Sun 10–6 ✋ Art of Old Poland gallery and Orthodox Art gallery each inexpensive; combined ticket moderate; both free Sun May–Oct; Thu Nov–Apr ❓ Photography fee moderate

Archdiocesan Museum

✉ 19 ul. Kanonicza ☎ 012 421 8963; www.muzeumkra.diecezja.pl 🕓 Tue–Fri 10–4, Sat–Sun 10–3 ✋ Inexpensive

PAŁAC BISKUPI

The bishops of Krakow have lived on this site since the 14th century, but this 17th-century building across the street from the Franciscan Church attracts attention today for its 'Pope's Window' over the main doorway. This is where the then Archbishop of Krakow, Karol Wojtyła, later to become Pope John Paul II, lived between 1963 and 1978. From this window he held his celebrated conversations with the students and faithful of the city.

✚ 8D ✉ 3 ul. Franciszkańska

PAŁAC KRÓLEWSKI NA WAWELU

Best places to see, ➤ 48–49.

PAŁAC KRZYSZTOFORY

One of the grandest buildings on Krakow's main market square is the Krzysztofory Palace, named for St Christopher and built in the 17th century. In the past it gave hospitality to kings and revolutionaries; today different kinds of culture co-exist on different floors. The cellar club, where you'll find the latest urban music and modern theatre, spills over into the arcaded courtyard in summer, while the upstairs Fontana Room with its fine stucco ceilings is the venue for regular classical concerts. The palace is also the headquarters of the Historical Museum of the City of Krakow, with a permanent exhibition about the culture and history of the city. Every December, the palace continues the tradition of displaying the best *szopki* or Christmas cribs, made by local adults and children.

www.mhk.pl

✚ 8D ✉ 35 Rynek Główny ☎ 012 619 2300 🕓 Museum: May–Oct Wed–Sun 10–5:30; Nov–Apr Wed, Fri–Sun 9–4, Thu 10–5. Closed Mon, Tue and 2nd Sun of the month, 1 Jan, Easter Fri–Sun, 1 and 11 Nov, 24–25, 31 Dec 🎟 Inexpensive 🍴 Courtyard café, cellar club (€)

PIWNICA POD BARANAMI

In the cellar of Dom Pod Baranami, at the far end of the main market square from the Krzysztofory Palace, the Piwnica Pod Baranami, or Alehouse Under the Sign of the Rams, was from 1956 home to Poland's most notorious cabaret. In its heyday, it was the scene of wild happenings devised on a shoestring and no one left until the early hours. Today, though the cabaret tradition continues on Saturday nights,

it operates as a slightly more sedate traditional vaulted brick alehouse where the atmosphere lends potency to the beer. The rest of the building houses other arts venues including one of Krakow's best cinemas (➤ 111).
www.piwnicapodbaranami.krakow.pl

✚ 8D ✉ 27 Rynek Główny ☎ 012 421 2500
🕒 Weekly cabaret Sat 9pm–last customer leaves; bar daily 11am–last customer leaves ✋ Inexpensive
🍴 Café/bar (€–€€) ❓ Book cabaret tickets in advance Mon–Fri 11–3 at 26 ul. św. Tomasza or phone above number

POMNIK ADAMA MICKIEWICZA
The statue of Adam Mickiewicz, Poland's most celebrated poet, has a prominent place in the Rynek Główny, though he never visited the city in his lifetime. Born in 1798, when the country was partitioned and had effectively ceased to exist, the writer of *Pan Tadeusz* was not only a Romantic poet, but also a political activist who wanted to see the resoration of the Polish nation.

He died in exile in 1855 while gathering a Polish legion to fight for his homeland and was buried in France, until his body was brought back to be interred in Wawel Cathedral. His memorial in the square, unveiled on the centenary of his birth, was taken down and sold for scrap during the Nazi occupation, but was recreated from original parts found in Hamburg after the war. It is a favourite meeting place of Cracovians, who have nicknamed him Adaś, and is garlanded on Christmas Eve by the flower girls of the Rynek Główny.

✛ 8D ✉ Rynek Główny between Sukiennice and Szara Restaurant
🍴 Many cafés in the square

POMNIK KOPERNIKA

'Give me a place to stand and a lever and I will move the Earth,' said Archimedes, but Krakow Academy's most famous student, Nicholas Copernicus, went one better and moved the Sun. Until he published *On the Revolutions of the Heavenly Spheres*, it was generally believed that the Sun went round the Earth (rather than vice-versa). Although, being nervous of the church's reaction, he did not publish his revolutionary theory until he was almost on his deathbed in 1543, his ideas began to be formed during his studies here in his father's home town, between 1491 and 1495. You will find his statue in the Planty, near the Collegium Novum.

✛ 8D ✉ ul. Gołębia/Planty

POMNIK KOŚCIUSZKIEGO

The mounted statue of Tadeusz Kościuszko takes up a commanding position on the slopes of Wawel Hill near the Coat of Arms Gate. He had a dramatic life as a main player in the politcs of his age on two continents. A soldier and engineer, he took part in the American War of Independence, fortifying Philadelphia and West Point and winning the friendship of Washington and Jefferson along the way. Returning to a partitioned Poland he led a continuing fight for independence, instigating the insurrection of 1794 in Krakow.

✚ 8E ✉ Wawel Hill ☎ 012 422 51 55; www.wawel.krakow.pl
🍴 Cafés below the hill (€)

POMNIK PIOTRA SKRZYNECKA

The anarchic Piotr Skrzynecki, instigator and leading light of the cabaret at the Piwnica Pod Baranami (► 90–91), was central to the cultural life of Krakow up until his death in 1997. His statue, seated at a table outside the Vis-à-Vis bar, is always decorated with a fresh flower, in memory of his lively spirit.

✚ 8D ✉ 29 Rynek Główny 🍴 Outside Vis-à-Vis bar

RESTAURACJA WIERZYNEK

Embodying Krakow's long tradition of hospitality in its many grand dining rooms, the Wierzynek Restaurant can trace its history back to 1364, when the prominent citizen Mikołaj

Wierzynek invited almost half the crowned heads of Europe and his own king, Kazimierz the Great, to a banquet. So well did the meal help defuse growing tensions in Europe that the king rewarded Wierzynek with a permit to entertain future important visitors to the city. Heads of state and celebrities (King Juan Carlos of Spain, the then American president George Bush and Steven Spielberg among them) have continued to come to enjoy the traditional Polish dishes – wild boar, roe deer and roast sturgeon with Polish crayfish are all on the menu.

✚ 8D ✉ 15 Rynek Główny ☎ 012 424 9600; www.wierzynek.com.pl
🕓 Daily 11–11 🍴 Restaurant (€€€), café (€€), cellar bar and grill (€).

a walk within the Planty

The medieval streets of the Old Town, lined with *kamienice* or grand houses, all circled by the leafy ring of the Planty, have remained unchanged since the city's charter in 1257.

You can combine this at the beginning or the end with the walk around Rynek Główny (➤ 64–65).

Beginning at the Wieża Ratuszowa (➤ 101), walk past Kościół św. Wojciecha (➤ 84), and turn right down ul. Grodzka.

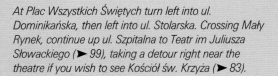

Ul. Grodzka is part of the Royal Route Poland's kings took to their coronations in the cathedral on Wawel Hill.

At Plac Wszystkich Świętych turn left into ul. Dominikańska, then left into ul. Stolarska. Crossing Mały Rynek, continue up ul. Szpitalna to Teatr im Juliusza Słowackiego (➤ 99), taking a detour right near the theatre if you wish to see Kościół św. Krzyża (➤ 83).

Branch out from the route at any point into the Planty.

Turn right along ul. Pijarska, passing Brama Floriańska (➤ 74–75) or walk through the Planty to the Barbakan (➤ 74), rejoining the route through St Florian's Gate.

Ul. Pijarksa borders the remaining part of the city wall.

Continue along ul. Pijarska. At the Czartoryski Museum (➤ 44–45) with its first-floor bridge to the Arsenal, turn left down ul. św. Jana. Turn right along ul. św. Tomasza.

At Plac św. Tomasza there is a little group of good restaurants where you can stop for lunch.

Cross Plac Szczepański and turn left into the Planty, passing Pałac Sztuki and its contemporary art cousin, Bunkier Sztuki. At ul. św. Anny, turn left and then right down ul. Jagiellońska past Collegium Maius (➤ 36–37).

Look into the courtyard at Collegium Maius to see the musical clock on the left-hand wall.

At ul. Gołębia turn right towards Collegium Novum (➤ 76), left at the statue of Copernicus (➤ 93) and wander through the Planty to ul. Podzamcze. Turn left.

Shortly, turn left up ul. Kanonicza, then cross Plac św. Marii Magdaleny and go left up ul. Grodzka back to the Rynek Główny.

Distance 3–4km (2–2.5 miles)
Time 3–4 hours
Start/end point Wieża Ratuszowa (Town Hall Tower) ✚ 8D
Lunch Café Camelot (➤ 104)

RYNEK GŁÓWNY

Europe's largest medieval square is little changed from when it was first laid out in 1320. The grand houses, or *kamienice*, on the square have been rebuilt after fires and according to fashion, Gothic giving way to Renaissance and baroque, as Italian architects became popular. Many are now shops and restaurants, so you can enter to see the remains of frescoes and vaulted ceilings. Several are still known by the emblems above their doors. 'Pod' means 'under the sign of' in Polish, so you can find Pod Obrazem (Under the Painting – an 18th-century Virgin Mary), Pod Białym Orłem (Under the White Eagle) and Pod Jaszczurami (Under the Fighting Lizards), as well as many others.

🕇 8D ✉ Rynek Główny 🍴 Many cafés and restaurants (€–€€€)

SMOCZA JAMA

Best places to see, ➤ 50–51.

STARY TEATR

The Stary, or Old, Theatre was left in ruins after World War II, but has now regained its 1905 art nouveau brio. Originally converted from several older buildings in the 18th century, it had already been enlarged several times. From the outside, the frieze by Józef Gardecki is striking, while the interior features flower-painted ceilings and images of the great names of Polish theatre.

www.stary-teatr.krakow.pl

🕇 8D ✉ 5 ul. Jagiellońska ☎ 012 422 4040 🕐 Theatre museum Tue–Sat 11–1 and from an hour before curtain-up 🎫 Moderate 🍴 Café Maska (€) 🕐 Mon–Sat 9am–3am, Sun 11am–3am

TEATR IM JULIUSZA SŁOWACKIEGO

The Slowacki Theatre, with its swirling cream and white architecture, was modelled on the Paris Opera by Jan Zawiejski. As well as plays, opera and ballet, it hosts international touring companies, so you may find something to entertain you here. **www.**slowacki.krakow.pl

➕ 9C ✉ 1 Plac św. Ducha ☎ 012 424 4525 🕐 Box office: Mon 10–2, 2:30–6, Tue–Sat 9–2, 2:30–7, Sun 3–7 ✋ Moderate 🍴 Café (€)

WAWEL ZAGINIONY

Situated in the ruins of the Renaissance-era Royal Kitchens,
the Lost Wawel exhibition is an imaginative attempt to breathe
meaning into what's left of the Gothic royal castle and a
9th-century chapel. You can see displays of the different phases
of building on Wawel Hill and archaeological finds from all

over the hill which help explain its complicated history, as well as computer simulations of some of the buildings which are no longer there and a model of the hill in the 18th century.

www.wawel.krakow.pl

🕂 8F ✉ 5 Wawel ☎ 012 422 51 55, ext 219 🕐 Apr–Oct Mon 9:30–1, Tue–Fri 9:30–5, Sat–Sun 11–6; Nov–Mar Tue–Sat 9:30–4, Sun 10–4; 1, 3 and 22 May, 15 Aug Sun hours apply; closed 1 Jan, Easter Sat–Sun, 1 and 11 Nov, 24–25 and 31 Dec ✋ Inexpensive, free tickets on the day Mon Apr–Oct; on Sun Nov–Mar 🍴 Wawel Hill cafés (€) ❓ Last admission 1 hour before closing

WIEŻA RATUSZOWA

The Town Hall Tower is all that remains of Krakow's Town Hall, whose first incarnation appeared in the square in 1316. After a fire in 1820 and a general clearing of the square, the tower was left as you see it today. Climb to the top for good views over three sides – there are inexpensive telescopes you can use, so take some 1PLN coins. At the top you can also see the mechanism of the the the former Town Hall clock. The current version is atomic.

🕂 8D ✉ 1 Rynek Główny ☎ 012 619 2318 🕐 May–Oct daily 10:30–6; closed in winter ✋ Inexpensive, buy tickets from Tourist Information Office on ground floor. Inexpensive photo permits extra 🍴 Café and theatre in cellar

HOTELS

Cracow Hostel (€)
With medieval window, carved beams and a view of the Sukiennice from the common room, this is one of the best locations in town. Breakfast included; air-conditioning.
✉ 18 Rynek Główny ☎ 012 429 1106; www.cracowhostel.com

Flamingo Hostel (€)
Party people like the discounts for local clubs at this hostel just off the Rynek Główny. Breakfast and internet included.
✉ 4 ul. Szewska ☎ 012 422 0000; www.flamingo-hostel.com

Francuski Hotel (€€)
A honeymoon favourite with 24-carat bathtaps and a belle époque ambience, though the original 1912 facilities have recently all been brought up to date. Parking; children and pets welcome.
✉ 13 ul. Pijarska 13 ☎ 012 627 3777; www.orbis.pl

Hostel Rynek 7 (€)
The walls are painted with poems and flowers and smokers have a view of St Mary's Church from their designated balcony.
✉ 7/6 Rynek Główny ☎ 012 431 1698; www.hostelrynek7.pl

Hotel Amadeus (€€)
This plush 14th-century town house near the Mały Rynek with a 17th-century painting of St Mary of the Rosary on its facade offers jacuzzis, fitness room, sauna and secure car parking.
✉ 20 ul.Mikołajska ☎ 012 429 6070; www.hotel-amadeus.pl

Hotel Copernicus (€€€)
A 14th-century facade in Krakow's oldest street hides a hotel with beamed ceilings and fragments of original frescoes in some bedrooms. However, it features all modern facilities, a small pool in the Gothic cellars and a roof-terrace.
✉ 16 ul. Kanonicza ☎ 012 424 3400; www.hotel.com.pl

Hotel Gródek (€€€)

Air-conditioning, sauna and modern bathrooms have been added to the antique-style furniture and stone fireplaces in this former 16th-century palace in a quiet place next to a Dominican convent.

✉ 4 ul. Na Gródku 4 ☎ 012 431 9030; www.donimirski.com

Hotel Maltański (€€€)

There's character and history aplenty in these three low, white buildings made into a boutique hotel on the edge of the Planty near the Franciscan church. It also offers business services and secure parking.

✉ ul. F. Straszewskiego 14 ☎ 012 431 0010; www.donimirski.com

Hotel Senacki (€€)

Knowledgeable, very helpful staff run a traditionally decorated but modern and comfortable establishment in a 14th-century building with lift. Showers, some baths. There's a café-bar in the 13th-century cellar, and breakfast is served in the ground-floor restaurant, with its beamed ceiling and carved stone pillars.

✉ 51 ul. Grodzka ☎ 012 421 1161; www.senacki.krakow.pl

Hotel Stary (€€€)

This ancient building has two pools, a fitness centre and a salt cave in its vaulted cellars, a rooftop café-bar and restaurant with views of St Mary's Church and a chic, designer feel despite the original frescoes in some bedrooms.

✉ 5 u. Szczepańska ☎ 012 384 0808; www.stary.hotel.com.pl

Mama's Hostel (€)

Free home-made cakes for tea on Thursdays at this central hostel in the 14th-century Kamienica Hetmańska (more rooms nearby), which is a regular on the list of the world's top five hostels.

✉ 4 ul. Bracka ☎ 012 429 5940; www.mamashostel.com.pl

Pod Różą (€€€)

Franz Liszt and Tsar Alexander 1 both stayed in the city's oldest hotel 'Under the Sign of the Rose'. It has been restored recently, with some original frescoes, marble bathrooms and heated floors. Gym with rooftop views.

✉ 14 ul. Floriańska ☎ 012 424 3300; www.hotel.com.pl

RESTAURANTS

Bar Mleczny Pod Temidą (€)

This is the real thing: an old-fashioned 'milk bar' (no alcohol), left over from Soviet times, but none the worse for that. You'll find hot, tasty, non-greasy and very fresh Polish food, served fast.

✉ 43 ul. Grodzka ☎ 012 422 0874 🕓 Daily 9–8

Café Camelot (€)

With its 13th-century stone walls, this has all the atmosphere of a cellar café, but at street level. The apple cake is what people come for, but you'll also find a good menu of light meals and salads.

✉ 17 ul. św. Tomasza ☎ 012 421 0123 🕓 Daily 9am–midnight

Chimera (€€)

Traditional dishes sourced from the aristocratic kitchens of the 19th century using seasonal Polish ingredients, including venison, goose, pike-perch and fallow deer.

✉ 3 ul. św. Anny ☎ 012 292 1212 🕓 Noon–last guest leaves

Chimera Salad Bar (€)

Down a passage a few doors from its parent restaurant, this Krakow mainstay is appreciated by vegetarians, and is as popular with ladies who lunch as with students – everyone is prepared to queue. Self-service salad bar, plus hot dishes.

✉ 3 ul. św. Anny ☎ 012 292 1212 🕓 Noon–last guest leaves

Galicja (€€)

Drawing its theme from the time when Krakow was capital of Galicia, the menu features lots of eastern European-style game dishes.

✉ 71 ul. Starowiślna ☎ 012 429 2607 🕓 Mon–Fri 11–10, Sat–Sun noon–10

Gospoda C. K. Dezerter (€€)

If you're looking for goulash with dumplings or spare ribs with plums, the Austro-Hungarian menu at this smart restaurant should hit the spot.

✉ 6 ul. Bracka 6 ☎ 012 422 7931 🕒 Mon–Sat 9am–midnight, Sun 10am–11pm

Hawełka (€€€)

A traditional, upmarket Polish restaurant with a salon – Restaurant Tetmajerowska – that features even more ambitious cooking. During its long history, it was once Krakow's premier delicatessen, Pod Palmą (Under the Palm Tree).

✉ 34 Rynek Główny ☎ 012 422 0631 🕒 Daily 11–11

Kawaleria (€€)

Serious cooking and impeccable service in a very smart restaurant with a cavalry theme, though the dishes are anything but retro. Good wine list. Inexpensive lunch menu until 4pm.

✉ 4 ul. Gołębia ☎ 012 430 2432 🕒 Sun–Thu 11–11, Fri–Sat 11am–midnight

Metropolitan (€€)

Kitchen drama as the chefs cook up a contemporary storm in full view. Excellent modern international menu and interesting, mainly New World, wine list. Popular expat hangout for breakfast.

✉ 3 ul. Sławkowska ☎ 012 421 9803 🕒 Mon–Sat 7am–midnight, Sun 7:30am–10pm

Morskie Oko (€)

Within its rough-hewn pine walls, you will believe you are in a mountain hut not a Krakow basement. It has a traditional rustic menu, charming staff, highlander menu and, on occasions, music, where guests are encouraged to join in.

✉ 8 Plac Szczepański ☎ 012 431 2423 🕒 Daily 12–12

Orient Ekspres (€)

All aboard for well-judged cooking inspired by the route of the Trans-European train, but including Polish specialities. Tables are arranged rather like a dining car but are better spaced.

✉ 13 ul. Stolarska ☎ 012 422 6672 🕓 Daily 12:30–11

Pod Aniołami (€€)

Sit in a Gothic cellar under a glass roof held up by massive stone columns, watching chef Tomasz Lis prepare old Polish recipes in a beechwood-burning oven.

✉ 35 ul. Grodzka ☎ 012 421 3999 🕓 Daily 1pm–midnight

Pod Krzyżykiem (€€€)

In this restaurant with romantic wall paintings you'll find an imaginative take on Polish menu favourites, such as blinis with smoked salmon and wild boar ham marinaded with cranberries.

✉ 39 Rynek Główny ☎ 012 433 7010 🕓 Daily noon–last customer leaves

Pod Osłoną Nieba (€)

The restaurant has stained-glass windows, greenery and a very resonable grill menu, but this site above the club Prozak (► 112) is famous for Krakow's favourite take-away next door, Kebab z Tradycją, which shares the same kitchen.

✉ 26 ul. Grodzka ☎ 012 422 5227 🕓 Restaurant daily 10am–midnight; take-away 10am–5am

Polskie Jadło (€€)

Keen staff serve traditional food based on the dishes of Poland and its near neighbours that's less rustic than most. Watch out for other branches in the Old Town.

✉ 23 Rynek Główny ☎ 012 423 8135 🕓 Daily 12–12

Restauracja Szara (€€)

Worth a visit if only to admire the beautiful old room and vaulted ceiling. The international menu speaks Polish, featuring dishes such as smoked reindeer tartar and butter-fried pike-perch.

✉ 6 Rynek Główny ☎ 012 421 6669 🕓 Daily 11–11

U Zalipianek (€)
Decorated in the style of the Malopolska village of Zalipie, these flower-painted rooms on the edge of the Planty are a pretty place to try a very standard range of Polish fare.

✉ 24 ul. Szewska ☎ 012 422 2950 🕐 Daily 9am–10pm

Wentzl (€€€)
A youngster compared with Wierzynek, this restaurant has been here since 1792. Chef Grzegorz Zdeb conjures up Polish and French specialities, such as wild boar fillet marinaded in wild berry sauce with honey liqueur and roasted garlic for his celebrated diners.

✉ 19 Rynek Główny ☎ 012 429 5712 🕐 Daily 10am–11pm

Wierzynek (€€€)
Top-flight service and food of consistent high quality in Krakow's oldest restaurant. Though the menu features traditional Polish ingredients and dishes, it has developed to appeal to contemporary tastes.

✉ 15 Rynek Główny ☎ 012 424 9600 🕐 Daily 12–12

SHOPPING

Alhena
A good selection of modern Polish glass, as well as the more tradition crystal, all hand-made in the Malopolska town of Krosno, sometimes known as 'little Krakow'.

✉ 1 Plac Mariacki ☎ 012 421 5496 🕐 Mon–Fri 10–7, Sat 11–3

Alkohole R7
Although it has an extensive range of vodkas in a myriad flavours, this shop is noteworthy for its beautiful old premises.

✉ 7 Rynek Główny 🕐 Daily 10–8

Ciasteczka Z Krakowa
Presentation boxes of handmade biscuits, cakes and chocolates typical of the city.

✉ 21 ul. św. Tomasza ☎ 012 423 2227 🕐 Daily 9–8

Cracow Poster Gallery

This is one of the best galleries in the country specializing in vintage Polish posters.

✉ 8–10 ul. Stolarska ☎ 012 421 2640 🕓 Mon–Fri 11–7, Sat 11–5

Delicatesy

Though it has the unwieldy official name of Podwawelska Spółdzielnia Spożywców, this is a handy place to buy Polish delicacies, including sweets, biscuits, sausages and cheeses.

✉ 34 Rynek Główny 🕓 Mon–Sat 7am–10pm, Sun 10am–10pm

Diament

Master goldsmith Andrzej Skibiński makes jewellery to order, and also stocks a good selection of more unusual silver and amber pieces.

✉ 62 ul. Grodzka ☎ 012 422 8707 🕓 Mon–Fri 10–7, Sat–Sun 10–5

Galeria Bukowski

Teddy heaven in a shop stuffed with bears.

✉ 1 ul. Sienna ☎ 012 433 8855 🕓 Mon–Fri 10–7, Sat 10–6

Galeria Dom Polski

Just off the Rynek Główny, this shop stocks a range of more unusual Polish arts and crafts than you'll find in the Sukiennice.

✉ 3 Plac Mariacki ☎ 012 431 1677 🕓 Mon–Sat 9–7, Sun 9–3

Galeria Ora

Displays the work of contemporary designers from in and around Krakow who produce high-quality, modern jewellery in silver, amber and unusual gemstones.

✉ 3/1a ul. św. Anny ☎ 012 426 8920 🕓 Mon–Sat 10–8, Sun 11–6

Galeria Rycerska

The full suit of hussar's armour complete with feathered wings may not for sale, but you will definitely be able to buy a breastplate or medieval helmet here.

✉ 5 ul. Szpitalna ☎ 601 476 683 🕓 Mon–Fri 11–7, Sat 10–3

Galeria Osobliwości

Its name translates as Cabinet of Curiosities and that is exactly
what this shop is, selling unusual objects, furniture and jewellery
old and new from all over the world. Customs may look bemused
if you buy the rhinoceros skull to take home.

✉ 16 ul. Sławkowska ☎ 012 429 1984 🕐 Mon–Fri 11–7, Sat 11–3

Krakowski Kredens

With a cold-meat counter that celebrates the Polish love of
all things porcine, this new high-class food shop also sells
biscuits, cakes, preserves, cheeses and other fine local produce
attractively packaged.

✉ 7 ul. Grodzka ☎ 012 423 8159 🕐 Mon–Fri 10–7, Sat 11–7, Sun 11–5

Księgarnia Camena

Worth a visit, not for the books, but for classical CDs by
traditional and contemporary composers.

✉ 34 Rynek Główny ☎ 012 422 6023 🕐 Daily 10–7

Polskie Szkło

Sparkling selection of traditional and modern Polish glass and
crystal, as well as a stock of high-quality Christmas decorations
year-round.

✉ 36 ul. Grodzka ☎ 012 422 5739 🕐 Mon–Fri 10–7, Sat 10–3

Sukiennice

The first place to look for souvenirs and jewellery, as well as all
kinds of Polish arts and crafts. Good quality and fair prices.

✉ 1–3 Rynek Główny ☎ None 🕐 Daily 10–8

Wawel

This shop, which sells the quintessential Polish sweets, has
branches all over the country. Treat yourself to the Królewski
Smak (Royal Taste) selection or experiment with chocolate-
covered plums, praline-centred *Michałki* or chestnut-flavoured
Kasztanki.

✉ 33 Rynek Główny ☎ 012 423 12 47 🕐 Daily 10–7

ENTERTAINMENT

If you love live classical music you will be spoiled for choice in Krakow. Occasional concerts are advertised with posters and leaflets, but many churches and historical buildings have regular events. Tickets are usually sold on the door. Here is a typical selection, although times may change according to season.

Chopin ✉ Pałac Bonerowski, 1 ul. św. Jana; Pod Gruszką Journalists' Club, 1 ul. Szczepańska; Teatr im Juliusz Słowackiego, 1 Plac św. Ducha ☎ 604 093 570; www.pro-arts.pl ◑ Many nights of the week at 7pm

Concerts and organ music in churches

✉ Kościół św. Piotra i Pawła, 54 ul. Grodzka ☎ 695 574 526 ◑ Many nights of the week, 5pm organ concerts, 8pm chamber music

✉ Kościół O. O. Bernardynów, 2 ul. Bernardyńska ☎ 695 574 526 ◑ Tue, Sat 8:30pm

✉ Kościół św. Idziego, 67 ul. Grodzka ☎ 695 574 526 ◑ Mon, Thu 7pm

Boro

Early on you can relax with coffee on leather sofas; excitement builds later with DJs and live music in this three-room, courtyard-level club in the Pod Baranami building.

✉ 27 Rynek Główny ☎ 693 922 010 ◑ Nightly 5pm–last customer leaves

Cracow Cinema Center Ars

Several screens on the site of Kino Sztuka, one of Poland's oldest cinemas, showing original-language films, both art-house and blockbuster, with Polish subtitles.

✉ 6 ul. św. Jana ☎ 012 421 4199; www.ars.pl; reservations – www.dokina.pl ◑ Daily, various times

Dom Polonia

Regular 80-minute Chopin piano recitals by well-known artistes or, at the same venue on Sundays, a 75-minute show of folk singing and dancing.

✉ 14 Rynek Główny ☎ 662 007 255; www.orfeusz.eu ◑ Chopin concerts Fri–Sat 7pm; folk show Sun 5pm

Entertain the Dragon

If you want to get a handle on the great Krakow cabaret tradition, but are defeated by language difficulties, get a satirical slant on the city at this annual summer-season dinner show, which lets English-speakers in on the experience.

✉ Centrum Sztuki Moliere, 4 ul. Szewska ☎ 602 772 265; www.stawowy.pl
🕐 Jul–Aug Fri 7pm

Filharmonia

Specializing in large vocal and instrumental works, this is the biggest philharmonic in the country, with a symphonic orchestra, mixed choir and boys' choir. It also stages concerts in Wawel Castle and the Collegium Novum.

✉ Filharmonia im. Karola Szymanowskiego w Krakowie, 1 ul. Zwierzyniecka
☎ 012 422 9477 ext 33, 012 429 1438 ext 33; www.filharmonia.krakow.pl
🕐 Ticket office Tue–Fri 11–2, 3–7, Sat–Sun 1 hour before performance

Harris Piano Jazz Bar

Polish and international live bands several times a week: includes jazz, both trad and modern, blues and other, newer styles of music in this packed and sometimes sweaty cellar bar.

✉ 28 Rynek Główny ☎ 012 421 5741, reservations possible;
www.harris.krakow.pl 🕐 Nightly 9pm–2am

Jazz Rock Café

This cellar club, with its crazy dancing and wild atmosphere, is a city legend.

✉ 12 ul. Sławkowska ☎ 511 433 506; 603 462 340; www.jazzrockcafe.pl
🕐 Daily 4pm–4am

Kino Pod Baranami

You'll find excellent movies from all over the world at this two-screen, art-house cinema in the Pod Baranami building.

✉ 27 Rynek Główny ☎ 012 423 0768; www.kinopodbaranami.pl
🕐 Daily 12–12

Krzysztofory Palace

In the cellar, electronica rules. In summer clubbers cool off in the courtyard bar. Above in the 17th-century Fontana room, you can hear the Cracow Philharmonic Quartet play Chopin and more.

✉ 35 Rynek Główny; enter cellar club from 2 ul. Szczepańska ☎ Classical concerts: 600 498 652, 501 638 750; www.classica.krakow.pl; cellar club: 012 422 2236; www.krzysztofory.pl 🕐 Classical concerts Sun 7pm; other classical concerts usually Wed and Sat; cellar club nights 5pm–last customer leaves

Opera Krakowska

Krakow's opera performs a repertoire of Polish and European classics on three stages: two on either side of the Planty and one in Nowa Huta.

✉ Teatr im Juliusz Słowackiego and PWST Stage, 22 ul. Straszewskiego ☎ 012 296 6262, 012 296 6263; www.opera.krakow.pl 🕐 Regular opera seasons, check with ticket office for performance schedule and times

Piwnica Pod Baranami

See pages 90–91.

Prozak

Krakow's core club experience, with local and international DJs playing for a smart crowd on three dance floors.

✉ 6 Plac Dominikański ☎ 012 429 1128; www.prozak.pl 🕐 7pm–very late

The Piano Rouge

Live music – pop, blues and standards as well as jazz – every night of the week in this sophisticated, three-room, red-carpeted, air-conditioned cellar club, bar and restaurant.

✉ 46 Rynek Główny ☎ 012 431 0333; www.thepianorouge.com 🕐 Sun–Thu 9pm–2am, Fri–Sat 9pm–4am

Showtime

Rock and pop for over-21s who make it past the zebra heads to the crimson seats.

✉ 28 Rynek Główny ☎ 012 421 4714 🕐 Fri–Sat 7pm–4am, Sun–Thu 7pm–2am

Kazimierz

Less than two decades ago, Kazimierz was almost derelict – a sad, broken-down memorial to its former inhabitants, the thousands of Jews murdered by the Nazis.

Today, synagogues have been renovated as museums and cafés and restaurants serve Jewish food and resound nightly to the music of *klezmer* bands. For an alternative, go clubbing with Krakow's young bohemians.

KOŚCIÓŁ BOŻEGO CIAŁA

The first parish church of Kazimierz the Great's new town, Corpus Christi Church was begun in 1342, but improved many times until by the end of the 16th century it became the vast Gothic basilica you see today. The highlight of the richly ornamented baroque interior added in the 17th and 18th centuries is a boat-shaped pulpit carried by dolphins and mermaids.

www.kanonicy.pl

✠ 20H ✉ 26 ul. Bożego Ciała ☎ 012 430 6290; 012 430 6294 ⊕ Daily, services 6:30am–7pm 👋 Free 🚌 Tram 6, 8 to Plac Wolnica

MUZEUM ETNOGRAFICZNE

This display, housed in Kazimierz's Renaissance old town hall, portrays the daily life and folklore of the people living in the countryside around Krakow, and is taken from some 80,000 items dating mainly from the 19th century. You'll find traditional Christmas cribs, examples of pagan festivals, beautifully embroidered Krakowianka folk dress and recreations of traditional flower-painted wooden houses, complete with butter churns and potter's wheels.

✠ 20H ✉ Ratusz, 1 Plac Wolnica ☎ 012 430 5563, 012 430 5575; www.mek.krakow.pl ⊕ Tue–Wed, Fri–Sat 11–7, Thu 11–9, Sun 11–3; closed Mon, 1 Jan, Easter Sat–Sun, 1, 3, 2 May, Corpus Christi, 15 Aug.

1, 11 Nov, 24–26 Dec  Inexpensive 🚌 502 to Plac Wolnica. Tram 3, 6, 8, 10, 40 to Plac Wolnica

MUZEUM INŻYNIERII MIEJSKIEJ

The Museum of Urban Engineering, situated in Krakow's former tram depot and bus garage, concentrates on vehicles manufactured in Poland and is a treat for lovers of old motorbikes and cars. Children aged five to nine can pull levers, switches and ropes in the modern interactive science area. Although not all the explanations are in English, there is enough to enjoy on a short visit. The display of old trams is closed for renovation.

✚ 20H ✉ 15 ul. św. Wawrzyńca ☎ 012 421 1242; www.mimk.com.pl ⏰ Jun–Sep Tue, Thu 10–6, Wed, Fri–Sun 10–4; Oct–May Tue–Sun 10–4 Inexpensive 🍴 Brasserie café/restaurant (€) 🚃 Tram 3, 13, 24 to ul. św. Wawrzyńca/ul. Starowiślna

NOWY CMENTARZ ŻYDOWSKI

Cross under the railway line on the far side of ul. Starowiślna to find the resting place of many of Krakow's eminent Jewish people, including rabbis, painters, professors and politicians. The New Jewish Cemetery was opened in 1800 when the Remuh cemetery closed because of lack of space. There's a memorial to those who died in the Holocaust to the right, just inside the entrance to the cemetery.

✚ 21G ✉ 55 ul. Miodowa ⏱ Sun–Fri 8–6; closed Sat, Jewish hols 🚋 Tram 3, 13, 24 to Miodowa ✋ Free ❓ Men must cover their heads to enter

PLAC NOWY

Though it's now at the heart of bohemian life in Krakow, and where many long nights of hedonism start, New Square today can seem rather quiet and faded. As 'Jewish Square' it was a busy place before the war, with a bustling market. The green Okrąglak in the middle, now used by fast-food stalls, was once a ritual slaughterhouse, and the square used to be the main trading place of the Jewish district. On one side of the square is ul. Estery, said to be named after Esther, Kazimierz the Great's Jewish mistress. Today there's a fruit and vegetable market most days, and a Sunday morning flea market, while the fast-food stalls offer huge, very inexpensive portions of *placki*, or potato cakes, and *zapiekanki*, a kind of Polish pizza on French bread, both with various toppings.

✚ 20H ✉ Plac Nowy ⏱ Daily. Stalls 8–4 🍴 Fast food daily 9am–2am (€) 🚋 Tram 6, 8, 10 to Miodowa

STARA SYNAGOGA

Best places to see, ➤ 52–53.

SYNAGOGA I CMENTARZ REMUH

The Remuh Synagogue, second in age to the Old Synagogue, is the only one in Krakow that regularly holds services. It was founded in 1553 by King Zygmunt August's banker Israel Isserles Auerbach, and named for his son Moses Isserles, a rabbi and Talmudic scholar, whose name was shortened to Remuh. Today no one ever sits where he prayed – a lighted lamp marks the spot. Despite wartime plundering, the synagogue's Renaissance collection box and late-Renaissance Ark survive, while the 17th-century bimah door comes from a synagogue outside Krakow. The rabbi is buried in the cemetery behind the synagogue. Closed to burials in 1800, this contains some of the oldest tombstones in Poland. During post-war restoration, some of the broken tombstones were erected alongside ul. Szeroka and now form Kazimierz's own 'Wailing Wall'.

www.krakow.jewish.org.pl

✠ 20H ✉ 40 ul. Szeroka ☎ 012 429 5735, 012 430 5411 🕓 Sun–Fri 9–6; Sat 9–6 for prayer and services only ✋ Inexpensive 🚌 Tram 3, 24 to Miodowa ❓ Female visitors should cover their shoulders, men their heads

SYNAGOGA IZAAKA

With a stucco cradle vault and Tuscan-style columns supporting the women's gallery, this baroque synagogue, built in 1644, is Kazimierz's largest. Legend tells us that Isaac Jakubowicz founded it after discovering treasure in his oven. Despite being despoiled in wartime, it still shows traces of 17th- and 18th-century wall paintings. Renovation is continuing.

🕂 20H ✉ 18 ul. Kupa ☎ 012 430 5577, 602 300 277 🕔 Sun–Fri 9–7 👋 Inexpensive 🚋 Tram 3, 13, 24 to Miodowa

SYNAGOGA TEMPEL

In contrast to the rather plain, white-walled restoration of Kazimierz's other synagogues, the interior of this progressive synagogue, built in the 1860s, is extremely colourful, with beautifully restored stained-glass windows and lots of gilt and Sephardic-influenced decoration. Britain's Prince Charles formally opened the Krakow Jewish Community Centre next door in April 2008.

www.krakow.jewish.org.pl

🕂 20H ✉ 23–24 ul. Miodowa ☎ 012 429 5411 🕔 Sun–Fri 10–6; closed Sat and Jewish holidays 👋 Inexpensive 🚋 Tram 6, 8 to Miodowa ❓ Female visitors should cover their shoulders, men should cover their heads

a walk around Kazimierz

As you criss-cross the streets of the former ghetto, you'll pass fashionable bars as often as haunting reminders of pre-war Jewish life. Much restoration is going on and the area is changing fast.

With your back to the Old Synagogue, walk down ul. Szeroka towards the far end.

You will pass Remuh Synagogue (➤ 118) and the cemetery's 'Wailing Wall' on your left. Roughly opposite is the Popper Synagogue, now a youth centre. At the end on the right, Klezmer-Hois (➤ 125) is where the ritual baths once stood. Gathered around this square are most of the Jewish-style restaurants in Kazimierz.

Taking the path by Klezmer-Hois, turn right down ul. Miodowa, cross ul. Starowiślna (watch out for trams), and carry straight on under the railway bridge to the New Jewish Cemetery (➤ 116) on your left. Retrace your steps, turning left on to ul. Starowiślna, cross and make your way down ul. Dajwór on your right.

The Galicia Jewish Museum (➤ 123) is active in keeping Jewish history and culture alive in Kazimierz.

At the end turn right on to ul. św. Wawrzyńca.

POToK
25

The Museum of Urban Engineering (► 115) is halfway down on your left. You could stop here for lunch or a snack at the Brasserie, which has a good reputation for its French food.

Cross back up ul. Wąska to ul. Józefa where you'll find the High Synagogue (► 122). Turn right up ul. Kupa to the Isaac Synagogue (► 119). Continue to the top of ul. Kupa.

You'll see the Kupa Synagogue, which dates back to the 1640s, on your right.

Walk back to the corner of ul. Miodowa and ul. Podbrzezie.

Here is the well-restored Tempel Synagogue (► 119).

Continue down ul. Miodowa away from the Kupa Synagogue and turn left down ul. Bożego Ciała.

The Corpus Christi Church (► 114) is a continuing reminder that at certain times Christians and Jewish people lived side by side in this area.

Leaving the church, turn right down ul. św. Wawrzyńca towards Plac Wolnica to the Ethnographic Museum (► 114–115).

Distance: 3.5km (2 miles)
Time: 2–3 hours
Start point The Old Synagogue ✚ 21H 🚊 Tram 3, 13, 24 to Miodowa
End point Plac Wolnica 🚊 Tram 6, 8 to Krakowska

SYNAGOGA WYSOKA

In the 16th century, when the High Synagogue was built, there were many ties between the Jewish people of Prague and Kazimierz, and this synagogue's design, much influenced by the style of those in Prague, is evidence of that. Called 'High' because the prayer hall is on the first floor, it originally had shops on the ground floor. Today it has a shop selling books on Jewish culture and music and CDs.
www.krakow.jewish.org.pl

✚ 20H ✉ 38 ul. Józefa ☎ Bookshop: 012 430 6889 🕐 Daily 9–7 💷 Inexpensive 🚋 Tram 3, 13, 24 to Miodowa

ULICA SZEROKA

Though its name means 'Wide Street', Ulica Szeroka originated as the main square of the ancient village of Bawjół, and is said to be the first site of the Krakow Academy, later renamed the Jagiellonian University. This is where everyone gathers in June for the open-air closing concert of the annual Jewish Culture Festival (36 ul. Józefa, tel: 012 431 1517, 012 431 1535; www.jewishfestival.pl).

✚ 20H ✉ ul. Szeroka 🍴 Many restaurants and cafés 🚌 Tram 3, 13, 24 to Miodowa

ZYDOWSKIEGO MUZEUM GALICJA

The highlight of the Galicia Jewish Museum is the exhibition Traces of Memory, which consists of photographs taken by the late British photographer Chris Schwarz, who was also the founder of this modern cultural centre. His pictures, taken over 12 years spent travelling around Poland with Professor

Jonathan Webber, who provides the commentary, document the remnants of eight centuries of Jewish life in Poland. The aim was to revive positive memories blotted out by the horror of the Holocaust. An inspiring and energetic man, Schwarz also set up a programme of events, including debates, other exhibitions, live concerts and talks, to keep the culture alive today and promote dialogue between faiths. His work continues.

✚ 21H ✉ 18 ul. Dajwór ☎ 012 421 6842; www.galiciajewishmuseum.org 🕐 Summer 9–7, winter 10–6. Closed Yom Kippur and 25 Dec 💺 Inexpensive 🍴 Café (€) 🚌 3, 6, 8, 9, 13, 24 ul. Starowiślna/ul. św. Wawrzyńca ❓ Many special events. Contact the museum for details

HOTELS

Hotel Abel (€)
Simple, clean accommodation and 1970s-style furnishings – a characterful place to stay. TV but no internet; showers not baths.
✉ 30 ul. Józefa ☎ 012 411 87 36; www.hotelabel.pl 🚊 Tram 3, 10, 13, 24 to Miodowa

Hotel Eden (€€)
All modern facilities, plus sauna, salt grotto and ritual Mikvah bath (open to non-guests and said to be the only one in Poland), as well as a restaurant serving kosher food.
✉ 15 ul. Ciemna ☎ 012 430 6565; www.hoteleden.pl

Hotel Ester (€€)
A traditionally styled hotel near the Remuh, Popper and Old synagogues. *Klezmer* bands in the restaurant at weekends.
✉ 20 ul. Szeroka ☎ 012 429 1188; www.hotel-ester.krakow.pl

Hotel Karmel (€€)
There's an Italian restaurant in the very old cellar of this 19th-century building, with traditionally styled rooms.
✉ 15 ul. Kupa ☎ 012 430 6697; www.karmel.com.pl 🚊 Tram 3, 10, 13, 24 to Miodowa

RESTAURANTS

Arka Noego (€)
A good place to get the typical Kazimierz experience: Jewish food, lace tablecloths and *klezmer* bands nightly.
✉ 2 ul. Szeroka ☎ 012 429 15 28 🕔 Daily 9am–2am, kitchen 11am–midnight 🚊 Tram to Miodowa

Bombaj Tandoori (€)
Rather unexpected in the heart of old Kazimierz, but you'll get a warm welcome and a straightforward Indian menu.
✉ 7–8 ul. Szeroka ☎ 012 422 3797 🕔 Daily 11am–midnight 🚊 Tram to Miodowa

Klezmer-Hois (€)

The Jewish-style food is good and the atmosphere terrific in this, the first and most cheerful of Krakow's *klezmer* restaurants. Music nightly; reservations necessary.

✉ 6 ul. Szeroka ☎ 012 411 1245, 012 411 1622 🕒 Daily 8am–11pm
🚌 Tram to Miodowa

Kuchnia U Doroty (€)

Good, plain, tasty Polish cooking for when you just want to refuel rather than get the full-on Kazimierz experience.

✉ 25 ul. Miodowa ☎ 517 945 338 🕒 Daily 10–9 🚌 Tram to Miodowa

Once Upon A Time In Kazimierz (€)

You'll be sitting at an old sewing machine under someone's old wedding dress, but this place is more about ambience than food.

✉ 1 ul. Szeroka ☎ 012 421 2117 🕒 10am–midnight 🚌 Tram to Miodowa

Rubinstein (€€)

This house is where a cosmetics empire was born – or rather Helena Rubinstein. The international menu here is a sign of a new, smarter Kazimierz to come.

✉ 12 ul. Szeroka ☎ 012 384 0000 🕒 Mon–Thu 12–10, Fri–Sun 12–11
🚌 Tram to Miodowa

Szara Kazimierz (€€)

Serving modern, light dishes such as mozzarella with strawberries and spinach and poached salmon with teriyaki sauce and asparagus, this restaurant/bar is the younger sister of the Old Town favourite (➤ 106).

✉ 39 ul. Szeroka ☎ 012 429 1219 🕒 Daily 11–11 🚌 Tram to Miodowa

SHOPPING

Blazko Kindery

Featuring contemporary designers working mainly in acrylic and silver, this place is right to call itself a 'jewellery art gallery'.

✉ 11 ul. Józefa ☎ 012 430 6731 🕒 Mon–Fri 11–7, Sat–Sun 11–6

Galerie d'Art Naïf

Here you'll find the work of real artists rather than the pale copies on sale in the Sukiennice. The owner, Leszek Macak, is one of Poland's greatest specialists in the field.

✉ 11 ul. Józefa ☎ 012 421 0637, 515 138 709 ◷ Varies, but generally Mon–Fri 11–5, Sat–Sun 11–3

Galeria Szalom

There's something rather romantic and particularly Polish about the modern works for sale at this contemporary gallery.

✉ 16 ul. Józefa ☎ 012 430 6505; www.kazimierz.com/artszalom ◷ Mon–Fri 11–6, Sat 11–3

Produkty Benedyktyńskie

Everything in this shop, including the cheese, meats, honey, teas, juices and wines, has been produced by Benedictine monks.

✉ 29 ul. Krakowska ☎ 012 422 0216 ◷ Mon–Fri 9–6, Sat 9–3

ENTERTAINMENT

B-Side

Indie rock, indie pop, riot grrl, electroclash…this club doesn't care so long as it's music.

✉ 16 ul. Estery ☎ 694 461 403 ◷ Daily 4pm–midnight

Ptaszył

You'll find a good welcome in this orange-and-blue-painted café hung with quirky little birds – the open fire in winter is a bonus.

✉ 10 ul. Szeroka ☎ 512 077 026 ◷ Daily 8:30am–last guest leaves

Stajnia

They're adamant they won't play techno or hip-hop, but if you like '80s and Latin music, this party bar is the place for you. The courtyard – now green and pleasant – was used in the film *Schindler's List*.

✉ 12 ul. Józefa ☎ 012 423 7202; www.pubstajnia.pl ◷ Daily 11am–midnight

Beyond the Planty

Outside the Planty, the circle of gardens and trees which replaced the old city walls, Krakow's residential districts of Kleparz, Stradom, Salwator and Podgórze also have a long history, interesting architecture and plenty of places of interest, while further afield you'll find green spaces, extensive woods and long views from mysterious mounds.

BŁONIA FIELDS

The vast Błonia meadow is a short walk from the Old Town, and is where Cracovians gather when the celebration or protest is too big for the Rynek Główny. As well as historic military parades and Poland's first football match in 1894, it was where Pope John Paul II said Mass and canonized new saints.

🚩 4D ✉ Between al.3 Maja and ul. W. Reymonta 🚌 114, 164, 173, 179 to Cracovia Hotel. Tram 15, 18 to Cracovia Hotel

CENTRUM JAPOŃSKI MANGGHA

The Manggha Japanese Centre, a dramatic piece of modern architecture across the Vistula from Wawel Hill, was founded by the Polish film director Andrzej Wajda to display the Japanese art amassed by the influential collector Feliks 'Manggha' Jasieński.
www.manggha.krakow.pl

🚩 18H ✉ 26 ul. Konopnickiej ☎ 012 267 2703, 012 267 3753 🕐 Tue–Sun 10–6
🍴 Restaurant (€) 🚌 Several to Jubilat/Most Dębnicki and Rondo Grunwaldzkie. Tram 1, 2, 6 to Jubilat/Most Dębnicki; 18, 19, 22 to Rondo Grunwaldzkie

DOM ŚLĄSKI

Best places to see, ➤ 38–39.

KOPIEC KOŚCIUSZKI

On a fine day you'll get an excellent view of the city and countryside from the top of this recently restored mound. Poland has a tradition of raising mounds, or *kopce*, to its heroes, and Krakow has four. This one, dating from the 1820s, is a memorial to the freedom fighter Tadeusz Kościuszko. You can find out more about him in the museum in the fortifications below.

www.kopieckosciuszki.pl

✚ 2E ✉ 1 al. Jerzego Waszyngtona ☎ 012 425 1116 🕐 Daily 9–dusk; also evening opening with separate ticket daily May–Sep dusk–11pm; museum daily 9:30–4:30 ✋ Inexpensive 🍽 Café with outside terrace (€) 🚊 Tram 1, 2, 6 to Salwator, then bus 100 from Salwator or 101 from Rondo Grunwaldzkie ❓ Separate ticket for small waxwork museum

KOPIEC KRAKA I KOPIEC WANDY

Across the river from Kazimierz in the district of Podgórze is the mound dedicated to King Krak, legendary king of Krakow. Believed to date from pagan times and once topped with a mighty oak, it is near in age to Wanda's Mound in Nowa Huta, said to be the burial place of his daughter. Krak's Mound is sometimes called Rękawka, because of the belief that the people carried soil in their sleeves (*rękawy*) to build it. Rękawka is also the name of an ancient festival, which today lives on as a fair held on the Tuesday after Easter on top of Lasota Hill in Podgórze.

Krak's Mound ✠ 22L ✉ Off ul. Lanckorońska 🚌 107, 139, 174, 184, 198. Tram 3, 6, 9, 13, 24, to Wielicka

Wanda's Mound ✠ 24J (off map) ✉ Off ul. Ujastek 🚌 117, 138, 142, 149, 125, 132, 136, 139, 163, 172 to Sendzimir Steelworks. Tram 22, 23

KOŚCIÓŁ PAULINÓW NA SKAŁCE

It's said St Stanisław, the patron saint of Poland, now buried in Wawel Cathedral, was murdered on the steps of the Church on the Rock in 1079, apparently for displeasing the king. The church you see today is baroque, built in 1733. Outside is a statue of the saint overlooking the pool of holy water into which his severed finger fell. The crypt contains the tombs of eminent Poles such as the composer Karol Szymanowski, the artist Slanisław Wyspiański and the Nobel prize-winning poet Czesław Miłosz.

www.skalka.paulini.pl

🚻 19J ✉ 15 ul. Skałeczna ☎ 012 421 7244
🕐 Church daily; crypt Apr–Oct Mon–Sat 9–12, 1–5,
Sun 10–12, 1–5; other times by appointment ✋ Free
🚌 124, 128. Tram 6, 8, 10, 18, 19, 22

KOŚCIÓŁ ŚW. KATARZYNY
Founded by Kazimierz the Great in the 14th
century, St Catherine's Church has suffered
more than its fair share of disasters, including
two earthquakes. However, it still stands as
a good example of Krakow Gothic. There are
15th-century murals in the adjoining cloisters
and the church's good acoustics mean it is
often used for concerts.
www.parafia.augustianie.pl
🚻 19H ✉ 7 ul. Augustiańska ☎ 012 430 6242
🕐 Daily, first service 6am, last 7pm ✋ Free
🚌 124, 128. Tram 6, 8, 10, 18, 19, 22

LAS WOLSKI

In this forest, the biggest nature area in Krakow, is Piłsudski's Mound, raised in the 1930s in honour of Józef Piłsudski, general and politician. West of the city and stretching between ul. Królowej Jadwigi and the Vistula, it has eight walking routes, a winter ski route and a bike route. You will also find **Krakow Zoo** here, with a petting zoo, as well as snow leopards, jaguars, a herd of pygmy hippopotamuses and lots more.

✚ 13H (off map) 🖐 Free 🚌 102, 134 (for the zoo), 152, 192

Krakow Zoo

✉ 14 ul. Kasy Oszczędności Miasta Krakowa ☎ 012 425 3551; www. zoo-krakow.pl ☎ Daily summer 9–7; spring/autumn 9–5; winter 9–3 🖐 Moderate

MUZEUM DOM MEHOFFERA

A real cradle of the Mloda Polska or Young Poland Modernist artistic movement, this house was the birthplace of Stanisław Wyspiański and home from 1930 of Modernist artist Józef Mehoffer, who entertained fellow artists here until he died in 1946. Mehoffer was a painter, printmaker, set and interior

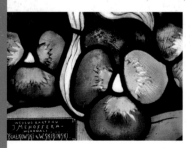

designer and rector of Krakow's Academy of Fine Arts, and he also created the stained-glass windows for Fribourg cathedral in Switzerland. He was also a keen collector, so this house gives an excellent impression of artistic life in Krakow between the wars.

✚ 6D ✉ 26 ul. Krupnicza ☎ 012 421 1143, 012 423 2079; www.muzeum.krakow.pl 🕐 Tue, Thu 9–3:30, Wed, Fri 11–6, Sat–Sun 10–3:30 🍴 Ważka café (€) ☎ 060 148 5055 🕐 Daily 10–9

MUZEUM HISTORII FOTOGRAFII

Poland's only photography museum lies across the road from Dom Śląski (► 38–39). As well as a fascinating selection of

equipment dating back to the earliest days of the medium, including a magic lantern apparently illuminated by what looks like Aladdin's lamp, it has a permanent exhibition of intelligently arranged early snaps of the city and its citizens, portraits of historical figures, including members of the uprising of 1863–64, and a good programme of temporary exhibitions.

www.mhf.krakow.pl

✚ 6B ✉ 16 ul. Józefitów ☎ 012 634 5932 ☎ Wed–Fri 11–6, Sat–Sun 10–3:30 🖐 Inexpensive 🚋 Tram 4, 14, 13, 24 to Plac Inwalidów

MUZEUM NARODOWE W KRAKOWIE

Best places to see, ➤ 46–47.

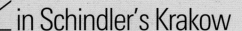

a walk in Schindler's Krakow

Many know the story of the Krakow ghetto from the film *Schindler's List* – these streets in Podgórze are where the tragic events actually happened.

Walk over Most Powstańców Śląskich from Kazimierz or take a tram to Plac Bohaterów Getta. Cross the square diagonally to the small museum in Apteka Pod Orłem.

By 1941, there were only 20,000 or fewer Jewish people in Krakow, though they had made up a quarter of the population pre-war. Forced into just 320 buildings in a new ghetto in Podgórze, they began to die of hard labour, overcrowding and deportation to the death camps. Tadeusz Pankiewicz's Eagle Pharmacy, the only Christian business in the ghetto, was a centre of resistance and help. There's a map of the ghetto on the street outside the museum.

Retrace your steps to ul. Na Zjeździe, taking care crossing the main road to ul. Lwowska, and turn right.

After the junction with ul. Józefińska, you will see parts of the ghetto wall on the right, with a memorial plaque at Nos 25–29 ul. Lwowska. Fragments also remain on ul. Limanowskiego.

At ul. Limanowskiego, turn right and walk back up the main road past the square to ul. Kącik. Turn right and walk under the railway line to ul. Lipowa.

You'll see Oscar Schindler's enamel factory on the left at the end of the block of 4 ul. Lipowa. Though he was no textbook hero, he negotiated with the Nazis to release

Jews from the nearby labour camp at Płaszów to work for him and in so doing, rescued more than 1,000 Jewish men and women from certain death. Today the building is being converted into a cultural centre, but is not yet open to visitors.

Retrace your steps to Plac Bohaterów Getta.

The installation of overturned chairs in the square by Piotr Lewicki and Kazimierz Łatak symbolizes the scene after the liquidation of the ghetto on 13–14 March, 1943, when the remaining Jews were deported or murdered in the streets.

Distance 2 km (1.25 miles)
Time 30 mins without visiting the museum
Start/end point Plac Bohaterów Getta 🕂 21J 🚃 Tram 3, 24
Lunch Ogień restaurant at Qubus Hotel (€€) ✉ 6 ul. Nadwiślańska
☎ 012 374 5100; www.qubushotel.com 🕐 Daily 12–8
Apteka Pod Orłem
✉ 18 Plac Bohaterów Getta ☎ 012 656 5625;
www.mhk.pl 🕐 Apr–Oct Mon 10–2, Tue–Sun 9:30–5; Nov–Mar
Mon 10–2, Tue–Thu, Sat 9–4, Fri 10–5 🛐 Inexpensive, free Mon;
audioguide inexpensive 🚃 Tram 13, 24 to Plac Bohaterów Getta

OGRÓD BOTANICZNY UNI JAGIELLOŃSKIEGO

The Jagiellonian University's Botanical Gardens are Poland's oldest and largest, dating back to 1783. About 15 minutes' walk from the Rynek Główny, they are a relaxing place to visit, if not particularly grand or even very ornamental, with wooded areas, ponds and various display beds. One of the two greenhouse complexes is the Palmiarna, which houses a group of palms several storeys high – stairs bring you level with the top fronds. The other, the Viktoria, is named after the *Victoria cruziana*

Amazonian waterlilies that grow in its ponds, their leaves as big as coffee tables.

www.ogrod.uj.edu.pl

✚ 11D ✉ 27 ul. Mikołaja Kopernika ☎ 012 663 3635 🕔 Daily 9–7 (9–5 winter months); glasshouses Tue–Sun 10–6; botanical museum Wed, Fri 10–2, Sat 11–3 💷 Inexpensive

POMNIK GRUNWALDZKI

The striking monument north of the Barbican commemorates the Battle of Grunwald in 1410 – a date that looms large in Polish history. Showing King Władysław Jagiellon triumphing over the Teutonic Knights, it was commissioned by the composer, pianist and prime minister Ignacy Paderewski to mark the 500th anniversary of the victory. The original statue was destroyed by the Nazis but re-erected in 1975.

✚ 9C ✉ Plac Jana Matejki 🚌 124, 152, 502. Tram 3, 4, 5, 7, 12, 13, 15, 19

STARY KLEPARZ RYNEK

If the splendidly restored main market square leaves you yearning for something more real, head north. Less than five minutes' walk away is the market at Stary Kleparz. It is typically Polish, with stalls selling pots, pans, garden seedlings, and lots of fruit and vegetables. You'll also find good local bread, cheese, sausages and honey, ideal for a picnic lunch.

✚ 9C ✉ 22 ul. Krowoderska ☎ 012 634 1532 🕔 Mon–Sat 7–7

HOTELS

Art Hotel Niebieski (€€)

Artistically modern, but emphatically not hard-edged, this hotel has some rooms overlooking the river and Wawel, bathrooms with heated floors and showers. Small but planning to expand.

✉ 3 ul. Flisacka ☎ 012 431 1858; www.niebieski.com.pl 🚋 Tram 1, 2, 6 to Salwator

Cybulskiego Guest Rooms (€)

Simple apartments with TVs, free WiFi, private shower rooms and kitchen facilities in a residential block in a quiet but central street.

✉ 6 ul. Cybulskiego ☎ 012 423 0532; www.freerooms.pl

Good Bye Lenin Hostel (€)

Down a quiet side street between the Old Town and Kazimierz, this great hostel has poker, film and live music nights, a garden, parking and decor that's a fun take on the Soviet years.

✉ 23 ul. Berka Joselewicza ☎ 012 421 2030; www.goodbyelenin.pl
🚋 Tram 13 to Miodowa

Hotel Pugetów (€€)

Smart, traditionally decorated boutique hotel in a former palace, with air-conditioning and parking. Restaurant in the vaults.

✉ 15a ul. Starowiślna ☎ 012 432 4950; www.donimirski.com

Ostoya Palace Hotel (€€€)

You'll find parquet floors and traditional tiled stoves in this well renovated 19th-century building. The ceiling in the restaurant exemplifies its romantic style. Showers rather than baths.

✉ 24 ul. Marsz J. Piłsudskiego ☎ 012 430 9000; www.ostoyapalace.pl

Pod Wawelem (€€)

Lovely location for the price, on the river between the Sheraton and Wawel Hill. The simple contemporary building has a rooftop café-bar with exceptional views, and fitness and steam rooms.

✉ 22 Plac Na Groblach ☎ 012 426 2625; www.hotelpodwawelem.pl

RESTAURANTS

Bar Vega (€)
Two spacious cafés offer vegetarian, salads and hot Polish dishes, but no alcohol. Summer gardens.

✉ 7 ul. św. Gertrudy ☎ 012 422 3494 ✉ 22 ul. Krupnicza ☎ 012 430 0846
🕐 Daily 9–9

Chata (€)
If there are several of you, pick one of the big 'feasts' for sharing that features a good selection of Polish dishes.

✉ 21 ul. Krowoderska ☎ 888 101 100 🕐 Daily 1–11pm

Gościniec Pod Zamkiem (€)
Try the wild boar steaks or duck in plum brandy sauce in this friendly restaurant. The *piwnica* here stages free cabaret-theatre.

✉ 11 ul. Stradomska ☎ 012 292 2212 🕐 Daily 10am–last customer leaves

Il Fresco (€€)
You'll find a Mediterranean menu with the emphasis on seafood in this 'piano restaurant' next to the Art Hotel Niebieski, with a garden but sadly no river views.

✉ 3 ul. Flisacka ☎ 012 431 2711, 012 431 1858 🕐 Mon–Sat 12–10, Sun 12–9. Piano concerts Wed–Sat from 7:30pm

Karczma (€)
Sit on a log and tend your own barbecue in this self-service pub by the river. The menu includes sausages *(lubuska)*, steak and *szaszłyk* (Polish kebabs).

✉ 14 ul. Kościuszki ☎ 012 427 0512 🕐 Daily 10am–midnight

SHOPPING

Grzegórzki flea market
There's more junk than treasure on display here on a Sunday morning – especially if you come late, but it's better value than many of Krakow's lower-end 'antique' shops.

✉ Plac pod Halą Targową, ul. Grzegórzecka 🕐 Sun 8–2

Excursions

For a change of scene, a visit to the medieval salt mines at Wieliczka takes barely half a day, and is much more fun than you might imagine. Another half-day and just a tram-ride away is the Socialist Realist suburb of Nowa Huta, whose steelworks have become the emblem of Soviet times. You can cycle to the monastery at Tyniec by following a pleasant riverside path along the Vistula, while at Częstochowa, you can see the country's greatest icon.

A visit to Auschwitz is not to be undertaken lightly, yet the camp will leave an impression that will last a lifetime. The mountain resort of Zakopane, by contrast, is a place of health and life, with green walks in summer, winter sports and a highland culture all its own.

AUSCHWITZ-BIRKENAU

The Nazi concentration camp whose name has become synonymous with the Holocaust is maintained as a memorial to the countless numbers who were murdered here in World War II. Many people feel obliged to visit, yet it's hardly an experience that fits easily into the average city break. Photographs are not allowed – remember the visitor standing next to you may have lost their whole family here.

The first slave labourers the Nazis brought to Auschwitz in 1940 were mainly Polish political prisoners. The terrible conditions soon killed many. Others died from starvation, criminal medical experiments or torture. Some were simply executed. By 1941 Soviet prisoners of war were being brought to the nearby camp at Birkenau, then, in 1942, the Nazis began bringing Jews from all over Europe for mass extermination.

After days travelling in rail cattle cars, they were unloaded and if deemed unfit to work immediately forced into 'shower rooms': the notorious gas chambers which killed 2,000 men, women and children at a time. It's thought that between 1.1 and 1.5 million died here by the time the camp was liberated in 1945.

You enter Auschwitz under the infamous gate with its slogan 'Arbeit Macht Frei' – 'work brings freedom'. In the blocks that once housed the prisoners, you can see photographs documenting their stories, possessions stripped from the dead – great heaps of human hair, shoes, spectacles, suitcases – and a film of the liberation of the camp. A

short journey away is Birkenau, where the wooden bunks would regularly collapse under the weight of the sheer numbers of skeletal prisoners crowded on each one, and where you can see the remains of the gas chambers and crematoria, as well as the railway line and unloading platform.

✉ 20 ul. Wiezniow Oświęcimia, Oświęcim ☎ 033 843 2022 (Mon–Fri 7–3); www.auschwitz.org.pl, www.um.oswiecim.pl 🕐 Site of the camp: daily Dec–Feb 8–3; Mar, Nov 8–4; Apr, Oct 8–5; May, Sep 8–6; Jun–Aug 8–7. Whole site closed 1 Jan, Easter Sunday, 25 Dec and for special events (posted on website) ✋ Museum free; headphones, film, inexpensive; English-language guided tours of 3 hours 30 mins (book ahead) moderate; longer study tours available 🍴 Cafeteria (€) 🚍 Oświęcim train station, from

here there are several local buses to the Auschwitz site 🚊 Oświęcim ❓ Visits are not recommended for under-14s. Allow at least 90 mins for your visit. Most spend much longer. An hourly shuttle bus covers the 3km (2 miles) between Auschwitz 1 and Birkenau 15 Apr–31 Oct, or you can walk (about 35 mins) or take a taxi

CZĘSTOCHOWA

The reason everyone comes to Częstochowa's **Jasna Góra monastery** – pilgrim and tourist alike – is the Black Madonna. This miracle-working icon at the heart of Poland's holiest shrine is unveiled daily with great ceremony. Already hundreds of years old when the Pauline monks brought her to their monastery in 1382, she suffered scars to her face in a 15th-century robbery attempt. Two of the many times she is said to have saved the country are when the hill of Jasna Góra was besieged by Swedes in 1655 and in the 1920 battle on the Vistula against the Bolshevik Russians. Make sure you visit the treasury museum and the other beautiful monastery buildings and walls.

Częstochowa Information Centre

✉ 65 al. Najświętszej Maryi Panny ☎ 034 368 2250; www.cestochowa.pl 🕓 Mon–Sat 9–5.

Jasna Góra monastery

✉ 2 ul. O. A. Kordeckiego, Częstochowa ☎ 034 377 7777; www.jasnagora. pl 🕓 Shrine daily 5am–9:30pm; holy icon uncovered at 6am, then covered and uncovered at varying times during the day. Museums open daily summer 9–5; winter 9–4 ✋ Expensive 🍴 Monastery café (€) 🚌 PKS coach station 45 al. Wolności, near train station and about 30 mins walk up al. Najświętszej Maryi Panny or 11 or 18 local bus 🚆 Częstochowa Osobowa ❓ You need to pre-book a tour to see the icon

Distance 140km (87 miles)

Journey time 2–3 hours by coach from Dworzec Autobusowy ☎ 034 379 1149; www.pks-czestochowa.pl; 90 mins–2 hours by train from Dworzec Główny ☎ 034 366 4789; www.pkp.pl

Leabharlanna Fhine Gall

KOPALNIA SOLI WIELICZKA

A tour of the salt mines at Wieliczka has become Poland's most popular visitor attraction. Serious mining of the valuable rock salt began here in the 11th century and hundreds of years of excavation have disclosed underground lakes and caverns so gigantic that today they house a cathedral, a ballroom and a concert hall, among other things. Salt miners down the ages seem to have inherited an artistic gene, too.

Your tour will take you past countless sculptures carved in salt. Much of the two-and-a-half-hour tour is an easy 2km (1.2-mile) walk below ground – the most difficult part is walking down 378 steps to the start. The deepest visitors go is 135m (443ft) below ground level, though the mine stretches down to 327m (1,072ft) and has about 3,000 chambers on nine levels. A lift brings you back to the surface.

✉ 10 ul. Daniłowicza, Wieliczka ☎ 012 278 7302, 012 278 7366; www.kopalnia.pl ✪ Apr–Oct daily 7:30–7:30; Nov–Mar daily 8–5; Easter Sat 7:30–1. Closed 1 Jan, Easter Sun, 1 Nov, 24–25, 31 Dec ✋ Expensive 🍴 Cafeteria above ground; simple restaurant at end of tour below ground (€) 🚌 Wieliczka Kopalnia, bus 304 from Galeria Krakowska; minibuses for Wieliczka Rynek from Krakow Poczta Główna (main post office) at junction of ul. Westerplatte and ul.Starowiślna, get off at junction of ul. Dembowskiego and ul. Daniłowicza in Wieliczka 🚆 Wieliczka Rynek, from Krakow main station ❓ Fee for taking pictures inexpensive

NOWA HUTA

This unlovely suburb of Krakow, begun on Stalin's orders in the 1940s, is today seen as a prime example of Socialist Realist architecture. The sights are very spread out so allow a lot of time (it's worth visiting the local museum first to get your bearings) or take one of the many tours from the city centre. Highlights are the Sendzimir steelworks and Our Lord's Ark, the Queen of Poland church, symbol of Polish resistance to Soviet rule.

✉ Museum of the History of Nowa Huta, 16 os. Słoneczne ☎ 012 425 9775; www.mhk.pl ⏱ May–Oct Tue–Sat, 2nd Sun of the month 9:30–4; Nov–Apr Tue, Thu–Sat, 2nd Sun of month 9–4, Wed 10–5. Closed every Mon, Tue after 2nd Sun, and every Sun but the 2nd Sun of the month ✋ Museum inexpensive, Wed free 🚊 Tram 4 to Sendzimir steelworks, ul. Ujastek or 15 to Plac Centralny ❓ While you're out this way, drop in on the collection of 150 planes at the Polish Aviation Museum on your way back ✉ 39 ul. Jana Pawła II ☎ 012 642 8700, 012 642 4070; www.muzeumlotnictwa.pl ⏱ May–Oct Tue–Fri 9–5, Sat–Sun 10–4, Mon (open-air exhibition only) 9–4; Nov–Apr Mon–Fri 9–4 ✋ Inexpensive, Mon free 🚊 Tram 4, 15 to Muzeum Lotnictwa

TYNIEC

The Benedictine abbey of Tyniec, said to have been founded by Kazimierz the Restorer around 1,000 years ago, is about 12km (7.5 miles) from Krakow. It has a commanding position on a cliff overlooking the Vistula. Although it has had a chequered history and fires and battles have afflicted the church and the monastery down the ages, the 15th-century Gothic buildings and their baroque interiors are being restored and the religious community has been revived. A short trip here makes a pleasant drive or cycle ride out into the country.

✉ 37 ul. Benedyktyńska ☎ 012 688 5200; www.tyniec.benedyktyni.pl
🕐 Daily, with services 6:30–6:30 ✋ Free – donation suggested 🚌 112

ZAKOPANE

This mountain town, 100km (62 miles) from Krakow in the high Tatras, is Poland's winter capital and a destination in its own right. It has been a ski resort for more than a century, and today it has 50 ski-lifts and 160km (100 miles) of runs, including some that are world-class and several that are floodlit at night. It's possible to ski here until May, after which the hiking season begins. Walkers have 240km (150 miles) of marked trails to choose from in the Tatra National Park. The town's prosperity was kickstarted in the 1890s by the artist Stanisław Witkiewicz, whose **Willa Koliba** popularized the pretty, rustic 'Zakopane style' of wooden buildings, and the place has functioned as a retreat for Polish writers and painters ever since. On a short visit you can explore the craft shops along ul. Krupówski, sample the *góralski* cuisine and watch rugged, axe-wielding highlander folk dancers.

Willa Koliba
✉ 18 ul. Kościelska ☎ 018 201 3602; www.muzeumtatrzanskie.pl
🕐 Wed–Sat 9–5, Sun 9–3 💵 Inexpensive
Skiing and hiking trails: Tourist Information Centre ✉ 17 ul. Kościuszki
☎ 018 201 2211; www.zakopane.pl 🕐 Mon–Fri 8–6 🚊 2 hours 30 mins–
3 hours 30 mins from Dworzec Główny 🚌 2 or more hours from Dworzec
Autobusowy, depending on traffic; faster and more expensive minibuses
from the same bus station
Tatra National Park Office ✉ Tatrzański Park Narodowy, 42 ul.
Chałubińskiego, Rondo Kuznickie ☎ 018 206 3799, 018 202 3288;
www.tpn.zakopane.pl 🕐 Daily Jan–Mar 7–4; Apr–May 7–5; Jun–Sep 7–6;
Oct 7–4; Nov–Dec 7–3

RESTAURANTS

Chata Zbójnicka (€)

Lamb is at the top of the menu of highlander dishes in this rustic place whose name translates as 'robber's hut'. A summer garden and a log fire in winter add to the appeal.

✉ ul. Jagiellońska, Zakopane ☎ 018 201 4217; www.chatzbojnicka.zakopane.pl ⏰ Daily 5pm–midnight

Karczma Czarci Jar (€)

Polish and traditional *góralski* dishes, accompanied by a highland band, are served in this new though rustic pine establishment.

✉ 11a ul. Małe Żywczańskie, Zakopane ☎ 018 206 4178; www.czarcijar.pl ⏰ Daily 4pm–midnight

Karczma Obrochtówka (€)

With a garden for summer and a folk band most evenings, this wooden restaurant is a good place to sample a typical range of *góralski* specialities.

✉ 10a ul. Kraszewskiego, Zakopane ☎ 018 206 3987 ⏰ Daily 12–10

Karczma Sabala (€€)

Sabala is located in an old hotel and is named after a famous folk-singer. The menu offers highland and international dishes.

✉ 11 ul. Krupówki, Zakopane ☎ 018 201 5092 ⏰ Daily 11am–midnight

ENTERTAINMENT

AQUA PARK

With various water slides and pipes, as well as lane swimming, a saline sauna and a climbing wall, this big leisure centre is a good choice for a children's outing.

✉ 126 ul. Dobrego Pasterza, Krakow ☎ 012 616 3190: www.parkwodny.pl ⏰ Daily 8am–10pm 🖐 Moderate 🍴 Restaurant (€) 🚌 128

GOLF

This 18-hole championship golf course is attached to a recreational complex with a driving range, shooting range, horse riding, winter skiing and snowboarding, and its own small hotel.
✉ 328 Miejscowość Paczółtowice, 32–063 Krzeszowice ☎ 012 258 8500, 012 258 8599, www.krakow-valley.com ☀ Daily 🍴 Expensive 🚊 About 1 hour by train or bus from Krakow main stations to Paczółtowice

MOUNTAIN GUIDES

The website www.pspw.pl lists contact details for qualified mountain guides who belong to Polskie Stowarzyszenie Przewodników Wysokogórskich.
✉ skr. pocztowa 289, 4 Droga na Wierch, 034–500 Zakopane

RAFTING

A trip on the Dunajec River through a spectacular gorge in the Pieniny mountains near Zakopane takes about 2 to 3 hours, depending on the water level.
✉ Rafts set out from the rafting marina at Sromowce-Kąty. Office: Polskie Stowarzyszenie Flisaków Pienińskich – Biuro Spływu, Sromowce Wyżne ☎ 018 262 9721; www.flisacy.com.pl ☀ Rafting daily Apr–Oct; ticket office Apr 9–4, May–Aug 8:30–5, Sep 8:30–4, Oct 9–3

ZAKOPANE SLOPES

For information about skiing and other mountain facilities around Zakopane contact:
Polskie Koleje Linowe (cable car company): www.pkl.pl has maps, prices and timetables in English for Gubałkowa, Kasprowy Wierch and others
Harenda ☎ 018 20 256 80; 018 20 640 29; www.harendazakopane.pl, click on Narciarska Zima for piste (ski run) maps and information in Polish
Nosal ☎ 018 206 2700; www.nosal.pl
Polana Szymoszkowa also has a geothermal swimming pool in summer
☎ 018 20 172 30; www.szymoszkowa.pl

Index

Street Index

Acknowledgements

The Automobile Association would like to thank the following photographers, companies and picture libraries for their assistance in the preparation of this book.

Abbreviations for the picture credits are as follows – (t) top; (b) bottom; (c) centre; (l) left; (r) right; (AA) AA World Travel Library.

All photographs by AA/A Mockford & N Bonetti, unless otherwise stated.

4l Wawel Castle; **4c** Tram; **4r** Wawel Cathedral; **5l** Café Europejska; **5c** Franciscan Church; **5r** Jasna Góra monastery, AA/J Tims; **6/7** Wawel Castle; **8/9** View of Kościół Mariacki (St Mary's Church); **10bl** Beer; **10br** Collegium Novum; **10/11** SS Peter and Paul Church; **11tr** Town Hall Tower; **12** Stary Kleparz Rynek; **12/13** Pierogi; **13tr** Salad and pancake; **13br** Chimera cellar salad bar; **14t** Café; **14b** Smoked sheep's cheese; **14/15** Pretzel seller; **15** Vodka AA/J Tims; **16b** Concert in SS Peter and Paul Church; **16/17t** Cellar bar; **16/17b** Rynek Główny town square; **18t** Botanical Gardens; **18b** Amber and silver jewellery; **19t** Stained glass in Mehoffer's house; **19b** Altar in Wawel Cathedral; **20/21** Tram; **24** Grand Dragon Parade; **25** Cockerel king of the Brotherhood of Riflemen; **28** City Tour golf cart; **31** Telephone, AA/J Tims; **34/35** Wawel Cathedral; **36** Courtyard, Collegium Maius; **36/37** Oriel window, Collegium Maius; 37 Library ceiling, © Jagiellonian University Museum; **38/39t** Identity papers; **38/39b** Exterior of Dom Śląski; **39** Needlework by imprisoned women on display in Dom Śląski; **40** High altar, Wawel Cathedral; **40/41** Wawel Cathedral; **42/43b** Painted ceiling in St Mary's Church; **43** St Adalbert's Church with St Mary's behind; **44** Lady with an Ermine by Leonardo da Vinci, © Princes Czartoryski Foundation; **44/45** Portrait of Chopin; **45** Meissen ceramics; **46** Wyspiański and Mehoffer stained-glass project, © National Museum in Krakow; **47** Wyspiański stained-glass project, © National Museum in Krakow; **48/49t** Inner courtyard, Wawel Castle; **48/49b** View across the Vistula River to Wawel Castle; **50** Dragon soft toys; **50/51** Dragon's lair, Smocza Jama; **52/53** Old Synagogue; **53** Prayer hall, Old Synagogue; **54** Knife in the Cloth Hall; **54/55** Facade in the Sukiennice; **55** Night view of the Cloth Hall and Town Hall Tower; **56/57** Café Europejska; **58/59** Benedictine Abbey at Tyniec; **60/61** Wyspiański stained-glass in the Franciscan Church, AA/J Tims; 62/63 Museum of Urban Engineering; **64** Adam Mickiewicz statue; **66/67** Stained-glass angel; **68** Alchemia bar; **70/71** Painted ceiling in the Franciscan Church; **73** Margrave's House in Rynek Główny; **74** Barbican; **75** St Florian's Gate; **76** Cab horses; **77** Collegium Novum; **78** St Andrew's Church; **80** St Barbara's church; **80/81** St Anne's church; **81** Franciscan Church; **82** Piarist Church; **84** Katyń Cross; **84/85** Archaeological Museum; **86** Pharmacy Museum; **87** Wyspiański Museum; **88/89** Bishop Ezram Ciolek Palace; **89** Pałac Biskupi; **90/91** Carriage in front of Krzysztofory Palace; **91** Piwnica Pod Baranami; **92** Adam Mickiewicz statue; **93** Nicholas Copernicus statue; **94t** Tadeusz Kościuszko statue; **94b** Piotr Skrzynecki statue; **94/95** Wierzynek Restaurant; **96** Grodzka street sign; **97** The Planty; **98** Under the White Eagle; **98/99** Slowacki Theatre; **100** Town Hall Tower; **101t** Lion base of the Town Hall Tower; **101b** Lost Wawel exhibition building; **113** Galicia Jewish Museum; **114** Ethnographic Museum; **114/115** Corpus Christi Church; **116** New Jewish Cemetery; **116/117** Prayer Hall, Old Synagogue; **118** 'Wailing Wall', Remuh Cemetery; **119** Tempel Synagogue; **120** Bookshop, Galicia Jewish Museum; **120/121** Window in Tempel Synagogue; **122t** High Synagogue; **122/123** Szeroka Street; **127** Grunwald Monument; **128/129** Kopiec Kościuszki; **130/131** St Catherine's Church; **132** Mehoffer's House; **133** Photography Museum; **135** Schindler's factory; **136** Botanical Gardens; **137** Grunwald Monument; **140/141** Jasna Gora monastery, AA/J Tims; **143** Auschwitz, AA/J Tims; **144t** Barbed wire, Auschwitz, AA/J Tims; **144b** Exhibition in Auschwitz, AA/J Tims; **145** Pope John Paul II statue, AA/J Tims; **146** Wieliczka Salt Mine, AA/J Tims; **147** Our Lord's Ark, Nowa Huta; **148** Benedictine abbey at Tyniec; **149** Country scene near Zakopane, AA/J Tims

Every effort has been made to trace the copyright holders, and we apologise in advance for any accidental errors. We would be happy to apply any corrections in the following edition of this publication.

Sight Locator Index

This index relates to the maps on the covers. We have given map references to the main sights of interest in the book. Some sights may not be plotted on the maps.

Dear Reader

Your comments, opinions and recommendations are very important to us. Please help us to improve our travel guides by taking a few minutes to complete this simple questionnaire.

You do not need a stamp (unless posted outside the UK). If you do not want to cut this page from your guide, then photocopy it or write your answers on a plain sheet of paper.

Send to: **The Editor, AA World Travel Guides,**
FREEPOST SCE 4598, Basingstoke RG21 4GY.

Your recommendations...

We always encourage readers' recommendations for restaurants, nightlife or shopping – if your recommendation is used in the next edition of the guide, we will send you a **FREE AA Guide** of your choice from this series. Please state below the establishment name, location and your reasons for recommending it.

_____

_____

_____

_____

_____

Please send me **AA Guide** _____

About this guide...

Which title did you buy?

   AA _____

Where did you buy it? _____

When? m m / y y

Why did you choose this guide? _____

_____

_____

_____

Did this guide meet your expectations?

Exceeded ☐   Met all ☐   Met most ☐   Fell below ☐

Were there any aspects of this guide that you particularly liked? _____

_____

_____

continued on next page...

Is there anything we could have done better? _____

_____

_____

_____

About you...

Name (*Mr/Mrs/Ms*)? _____

Address _____

_____

_____ Postcode _____

Daytime tel nos _____

Email _____

Please only give us your mobile phone number or email if you wish to hear from us about
other products and services from the AA and partners by text or mms, or email.

Which age group are you in?
Under 25 ☐   25–34 ☐   35–44 ☐   45–54 ☐   55–64 ☐   65+ ☐

How many trips do you make a year?
Less than one ☐   One ☐   Two ☐   Three or more ☐

Are you an AA member? Yes ☐   No ☐

About your trip...

When did you book? m m / y y

How long did you stay? _____

Was it for business or leisure? _____

Did you buy any other travel guides f

If yes, which ones? _____

_____

Thank you for taking the time to comp
as possible, and remember, you do no

| **AA** Travel Insurance call 0